Waltham Forest Libraries

Please return this item by the last date stamped. The loan may be renewed unless required by another customer.

Jan 24		

D1362484

www.**davidficklingbooks**.com

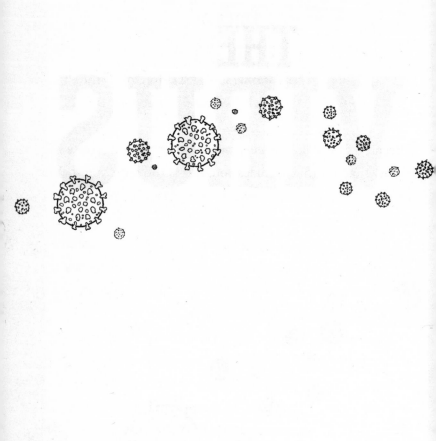

Foreword
by Paul Nurse

Nobel Prize-winning biologist, director of the
Francis Crick Institute, London

Because of coronavirus everyone has become interested in viruses, and if that includes you, this is the book you should read. SARS-CoV-2 coronavirus has changed the world for everyone, yet most of us only have a hazy idea of what viruses are. *The Virus* will tell you all about them. It is the essential introduction to these extraordinary life forms – the most abundant on our planet – that have a huge impact on the rest of the living world, including ourselves.

By reading this book you will discover that viruses are unbelievably small and that they can only make copies of themselves by invading the cells of other living organisms, in order to make hundreds, or even thousands, of copies of themselves. They are the ultimate parasite! The COVID-19 virus, like many of the other viruses that invade our bodies, can make us feel either mildly or, sometimes, very seriously ill. If we sneeze or cough, the virus is transmitted in water droplets and can infect someone else, and if this spread occurs rapidly it can lead to an epidemic or even a pandemic.

This book will inform you about how we can combat coronavirus, and where the virus comes from, but it will also tell you about many other viruses: ones that attack bacteria so they can no longer infect you, others that help bacteria make oxygen in the oceans, and yet more that might even help deal with climate change.

Reading this book is an adventure, an exciting journey through the strange world of viruses. It is easy to read, witty and humorous, informative and accurate, wonderfully illustrated. It shows how our immune systems combat viruses, how vaccines work, and maps out how we can deal better with pandemics in the future. If you want to know about viruses and coronavirus in particular, this is the book for you.

Jonathan Stoye FRS, virologist and senior group leader at the Francis Crick Institute, says:
'Although there are more viral particles on Earth than stars in the universe, over the past six months one particular kind, the SARS-CoV-2 coronavirus, has imposed itself on our way of life. This book tells us how and why in a clear and accurate manner, readily understandable by all.'

Professor Stoye is the scientific consultant and fact-checker for *The Virus*.

THE
VIRUS

Ben Martynoga

Illustrated by Moose Allain

David Fickling Books
31 Beaumont Street
Oxford OX1 2NP, UK

First published in Great Britain in 2020 by
David Fickling Books,
31 Beaumont Street,
Oxford, OX1 2NP

Text © Ben Martynoga, 2020
Illustrations © Moose Allain, 2020
Foreword © Paul Nurse, 2020

978-1-78845-210-6

3 5 7 9 10 8 6 4 2

Papers used by David Fickling Books are from well-managed forests and other
responsible sources.

DAVID FICKLING BOOKS Reg. No. 8340307

A CIP catalogue record for this book is available from the British Library.

Printed and bound in Great Britain by Clays, Ltd, Elcograf S.p.A.

The SARS-CoV-2 coronavirus that causes the COVID-19 illness is totally new to our world. Until November 2019 it hadn't infected a single person, which means there's still a lot that we don't know about it. But scientists and doctors all over the world have launched a massive combined effort to find out how the virus works and – crucially – what they might do to stop it harming people. Knowledge about the virus really is changing all the time – which is exactly how science works – so while the facts in this book have all been carefully checked, some things may change before publication.

Contents

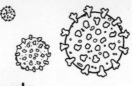

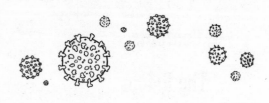

There are millions of different kinds of virus in the world, and only a very small fraction of them can infect humans. Coronavirus is a term used to describe a large group of different viruses that can cause diseases in mammals and birds.

SARS-CoV-2 is the full name for one specific species of coronavirus that causes the illness COVID-19.

Throughout this book we refer to the SARS-CoV-2 virus as the COVID-19 virus.

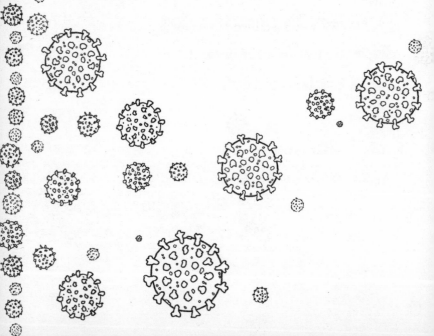

The Riddle

What is smaller than a speck of dust but more terrifying than any monster?

What doesn't have muscles but does have the power to stop all human activity?

What can't move itself an inch but can travel round the world in days?

What has no brain but is cleverer than any scientist?

What wears a crown but definitely isn't a king or a queen?

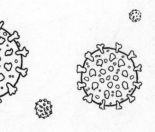

Hang on a minute. I'm not so sure about this riddle. You're tiny and brainless – and you can't even squirm or bite – why should we be scared of you?

Hey, less of the insults. I am scary. In 2020 I spread throughout your world and caused mass panic. I killed many thousands of people, overwhelmed hospitals and brought most of your world to a grinding halt.

OK, good point. We should be scared of you. You're an evil little scumbag.

No need to get personal. I'm not actually evil. I'm just a virus, remember? I can't think. I don't *want* to hurt anyone. I can't really *want* anything at all. Compared to you, I'm not much more than a little collection of chemicals. Really, I just *am*.

If I'm totally honest, I'm pretty scared of you too. Rumour has it your bodies are expert at spotting us viruses, hunting us down and sending us packing.

Yup, that's all thanks to our incredible immune systems. Plus, we can destroy you before you even get inside us – all it takes is a bar of soap!

Sad but true. In fact, left out on my own I'm actually quite fragile. And that soap stuff ... eughhh!

There's also that thing you humans call science. We humble viruses can't understand what that is. But we definitely don't like it.

Yeah, too right. Once our scientists develop a vaccine, you'd better reconsider your 'plans' for world domination. And you can tell all those other little viruses that harm people – we're coming for the lot of you.

Now you're getting a bit carried away. First, we viruses are EVERYWHERE. Oceans? Check. Forests? Check. Parched deserts? Check. Boiling-hot volcanic geysers? Check. Your bedroom? Definitely. We can infect all kinds of living things and we've got them all surrounded and outnumbered – including you! And, believe it or not, we actually help make the air you breathe and the soil plants grow in. Get rid of us, and most of the living world would simply collapse.

Second, some viruses might do nasty and painful things to humans, and most other living things too, but don't panic too much, only a tiny fraction of the world's viruses can infect people and there are some viruses that actually help you stay healthy. And anyway, it's not in our best interests to wipe you pesky humans off the face of the Earth altogether.

Confused already? It's not surprising. Viruses really are a whole set of riddles. How can they be bad and good? Deadly and essential? If they're so small and fragile, how can they cause such havoc? And how can we call them clever when they're just a bunch of dumb little chemical molecules?

So let's try to make sense of these mysterious viruses. Since we really do have to share our world with them and the nasty diseases they cause, we'd better find out all we can about what they are, how they live and how they spread.

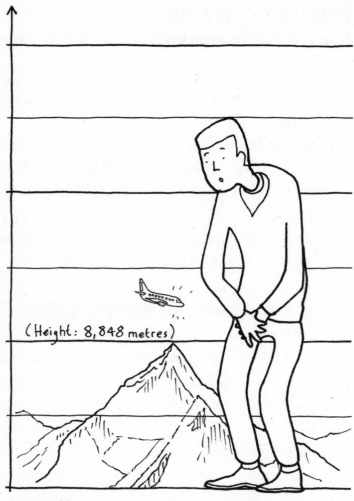

Chapter One

What the Heck is a Virus?
And how can it possibly wear a crown?

You'll already have gathered that viruses are very small. But the word 'small' doesn't begin to cover it. Viruses are mind-bendingly tiny.

Hold your hand up to the light. Can you spot some extremely fine hairs on the back of your fingers? They're about the narrowest thing you can see without a magnifying glass. You could line up 50 of them side by side and they'd still only fill up a millimetre on your ruler. Those hairs are small, but they're massive compared to a virus.

If a coronavirus drifted in and landed on one of those hairs, it'd be the equivalent of a flea hopping onto the trunk of a big old oak tree.

Now, hold on to that image of the blown-up coronavirus. How big would that make your whole body? Well, the actual size of the virus is 100 nanometres* across. If we blow it up to flea size (1.5 mm), it'll be 15,000 times bigger. And if we blow you up by the same proportion, supposing you're 1.5 metres tall in the normal-sized world, that would make you 22.5 km tall in our blown-up world!

*A nanometre is really minuscule. There are one million of them in a millimetre.

Your head would be way up in the stratosphere, nearly three times higher than the peak of Mount Everest. Aeroplanes might accidentally hit you where it hurts.

And this brings us to one of the most mysterious and confusing of all the riddles about viruses like the COVID-19 virus. How can the equivalent of a flea biting an enormous giant, with its head way up above the clouds, send that giant to bed with a fever? And how could it possibly kill such a magnificently huge human being?

If that makes viruses sound even more potent than the deadliest poison, that's because they can be. If we don't stop them in their tracks, that is.

Here's their trick. Unlike any poison we know of, when viruses get inside a body they multiply like crazy. That's basically what they exist to do. They're hell-bent on multiplying. Within a matter of days, one virus can turn into hundreds of millions of identical viruses. These copies can then spread through our bodies, making us ill and potentially infecting other people.

Sounds scary? Frankly, it is scary. But hang on in there, because we giants do have some highly impressive ways of fighting back. Before we get to those defences, though, let's look at what a virus actually is.

First things first: viruses are not cells.

Cells are what our bodies are made of. There are billions and billions of them, all working together to make each of your different organs – your heart, lungs, brain, skin and everything else. Each of those cells is a little living being in its own right.

In fact, all living things – apart from viruses – are based on cells. Animals and plants and many fungi are also made from lots of cells, while bacteria and other microbes are just single cells. We use the word 'germ' (or 'pathogen') to describe anything – a bacteria, a fungus, a protist* or a virus – that can infect us and make us ill. Except for the viruses, all of these are cells.

Viruses aren't just simpler than cells, they're less independent. Cells can make their own parts, produce the energy they need and actually make complete copies of themselves. Viruses can't – at least, they can't do it on their own. Instead, they're the ultimate parasites. In order to survive and multiply, they rely completely on the cells of the other living things they infect.

The COVID-19 coronavirus is a fairly typical example of

* Protists are organisms that aren't plants, animals, bacteria, fungi or viruses. That includes slime moulds, algae and various parasites, like the ones that cause malaria.

a virus. At its centre is a string of genes. You can think of these genes as working a bit like a set of computer programs that tell a robot exactly what it has to do in order to build and then operate another robot. Something as big and complex as a human being needs a lot of genes to build and run it: that's why each of your cells contains about 22,000 of these gene-based 'instructions'.

Our genes, and the genes of most other life forms, including many viruses, are made of a chemical substance called deoxyribonucleic acid. That's a bit of a mouthful, so it's usually shortened to DNA. The coronavirus's genes are made from a similar chemical substance called ribonucleic acid, or RNA. Viruses have far fewer genes than we do: the COVID-19 virus only has 29 of them, but that's enough to take complete control of the cells they infect and tell those cells precisely how to build lots and lots of new viruses.

Come and see what I'm made of...

ON THE OUTSIDE: The **membrane envelope** is a round bubble made from an oil-like substance called lipid.

It is studded with three different kinds of protein: the **spike**, **envelope** and **membrane** proteins.

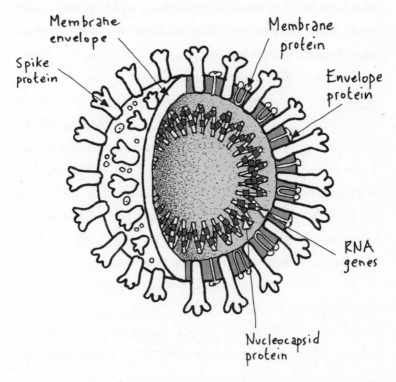

Membrane envelope

Spike protein

Membrane protein

Envelope protein

RNA genes

Nucleocapsid protein

ON THE INSIDE: The virus's all-important genes are part of one very long but very thin molecule of **RNA**. **Nucleocapsid** proteins stick onto the RNA and coil it up, so it fits inside the virus.

Coronaviruses hate soap because it's very good at dissolving lipids, destroying their membrane envelopes. The lipid in the virus's envelope layer is exactly the same stuff that makes up the membrane that surrounds and protects each of the cells in our bodies. But some viruses have no lipids in their outer shells; they just have proteins. However it's made a virus's outer shell protects its genes and gives it its distinctive shape.

Aren't you going to tell them about my crown?

Good point! Corona means 'crown' in Latin. And when scientists first used powerful microscopes to create images of coronaviruses, they saw a kind of ring, with loads of spikes sticking out. If you squint, it looks a bit like a crown.

And these spikes are seriously important for the coronavirus's way of life. Just as a house has its own key, which fits just one matching lock, each kind of virus has its own specific way of 'opening the door' and getting inside the cells it likes to infect.

The COVID-19 virus's spike proteins are its key, and the lock is a protein found on the outside of its favourite cells – scientists call it ACE2. Many of the cells in our bodies have

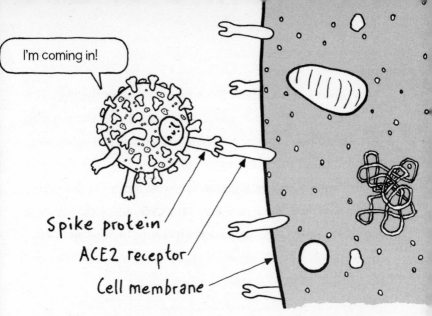

Spike protein
ACE2 receptor
Cell membrane

ACE2 embedded in the membrane that surrounds them, including the cells in our noses, throats, windpipes (tracheas) and lungs, which is where the COVID-19 virus usually tries to infect us first.

Coronaviruses are so small that they can easily get into our airways. We might touch an infected surface and the viruses stick to our skin. If we then touch our face, the viruses on our fingers can transfer into our mouth or nose. Or we could even breathe in viruses suspended in the air that an infected person has coughed out. Once they're inside the body, and the coronavirus bumps into a cell with the ACE2 protein, the coronavirus's spike 'key' can fit snugly into the cell's ACE2 protein 'lock'. Then comes the nasty bit.

Because there isn't really a 'door' attached to the ACE2

'lock', the virus uses the 'key' to confirm it's got the right cell and then basically tears a hole and fuses its membrane with the cell's. Then it pours its RNA genes directly into the cell. Help!

Having a stranger barging into your home is disturbing for anyone. But, for a cell, having a virus force its way in is especially traumatic, because it's likely to change that cell's life for ever. In fact, some of them never recover from the experience, as we'll see in the next chapter.

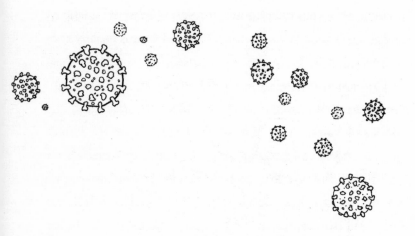

Chapter Two
The Ultimate Hijack
How the virus takes charge of our cells

Ready to do something a bit weird?

I hope so, because we're going to shrink ourselves down until we're about the size of a coronavirus. That means we will be 15 million times smaller than we are now, and about one hundred times smaller than a cell. That way we can actually get inside one of the cells on the inside of someone's throat and see how the virus works. Hold tight, it's going to be quite a ride.

Everyone OK? Going through the shrinker can feel strange and kind of disorientating . . .

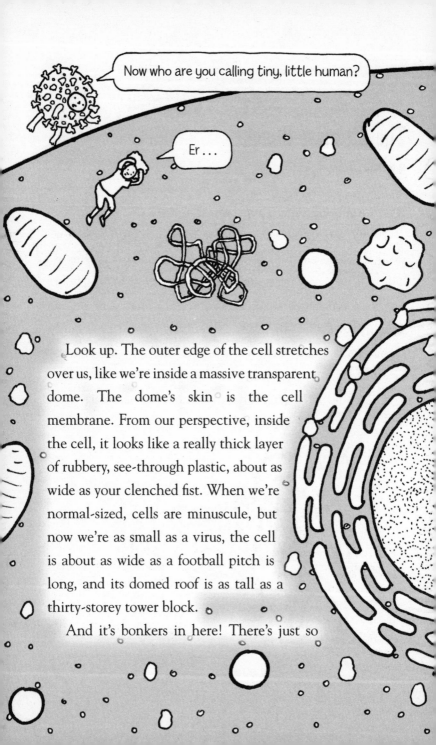

Now who are you calling tiny, little human?

Er...

Look up. The outer edge of the cell stretches over us, like we're inside a massive transparent dome. The dome's skin is the cell membrane. From our perspective, inside the cell, it looks like a really thick layer of rubbery, see-through plastic, about as wide as your clenched fist. When we're normal-sized, cells are minuscule, but now we're as small as a virus, the cell is about as wide as a football pitch is long, and its domed roof is as tall as a thirty-storey tower block.

And it's bonkers in here! There's just so

much going on. Everything around us seems to be moving and vibrating. We can actually see individual molecules – a mad array of blob-shaped balls, tangled strings and all kinds of other unusual shapes.

Even though we are massively shrunken, most of these molecules are smaller than us, but they're flying around everywhere, bumping into each other (mind they don't hit you!). Molecules are also changing each other: chemical reactions are happening all the time. This cell, like all our cells, is constantly busy: building new parts, patching things up, making energy and getting rid of its waste. That's how our cells keep themselves ticking over and how *we* stay healthy.

But look over there! There's the coronavirus forcing its way in. It's made a hole in the cell membrane and now it's fusing its own membrane with the cell's.

That's how it delivers its RNA genes: it basically merges with the cell – think of a small soap bubble joining on to a bigger bubble to make one single bubble.

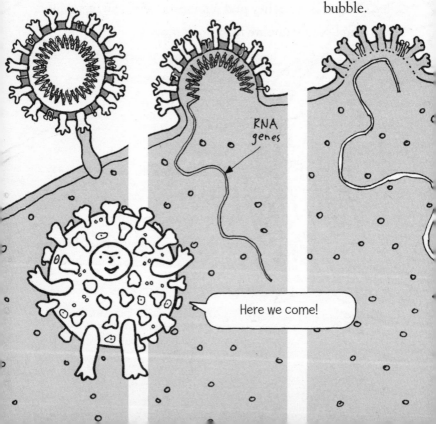

RNA genes

Here we come!

As this happens the virus's outer envelope breaks open and what was inside the virus – the RNA, holding those crucial virus-building instructions – is now inside the cell . . . Stand back! Here comes that long string of genes now, wriggling and writhing towards us like a big, fat and incredibly long snake*. And that gene snake seems to know what it's doing . . .

Deeper inside the cell, you might already have noticed lots of beachball-sized things whirring away busily. The virus's RNA is making a beeline towards one of them. They're called ribosomes, and they play a crucial role in the life of all cells. Including the one we're in right now.

* To us while we're tiny it looks about 3 cm wide and, stretched out, it would be about 135 m long.

Ribosomes work a little bit like tiny 3D printers: they take in information and they turn it into solid three-dimensional objects that do stuff*. Instead of computer code, they get their information from the genetic code stored in genes.

The objects the ribosomes 'print' are protein molecules. All living things urgently need proteins, because they are the cell's most important workers. Every cell contains thousands of different kinds of proteins. These molecules are the things that build structures, control chemical reactions, send and receive signals, make energy, recycle waste and much, much more.

Viruses need proteins too. Apart from its RNA genes and the lipids in its membrane envelope, that's what the coronavirus is made from. The virus has infected the cell we're inside now, because it wants to reproduce itself in order to make lots of new viruses. But it has a problem: the virus doesn't have its own ribosomes – no virus does – so it can't make any of its own proteins. Instead, viruses get the cell's ribosomes to make proteins for them.

Look, the virus's RNA snake has reached a ribosome. The ribosome seems pleased to see it! It sucks the virus genes in, like a small round mouth hoovering up a giant piece of

---

* Ribosomes make proteins as long, chain-like molecules, which then fold up to become solid 3D shapes. Imagine a piece of sticky tape getting tangled into a ball of loops.

spaghetti. And there – out of the top of the ribosome – new protein molecules are starting to take shape. But instead of the proteins the *cell needs*, those are the proteins the *virus needs*.

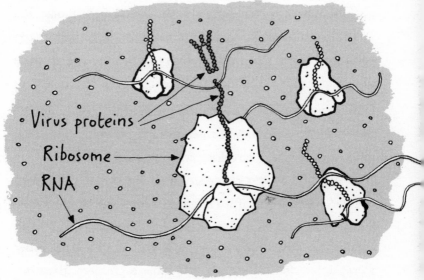

Virus proteins
Ribosome
RNA

The ribosome is reading the virus's genes and pushing out new proteins. It makes two large protein molecules first, then snips them up into 16 different, smaller proteins, which immediately get to work taking over the cell's operations. And one of their first tasks is to force the cell to make lots of copies of the virus's RNA genes.

Every new virus needs a full set of RNA genes, but copying genes is one of the other vital things no virus can do for itself.

So that's exactly what some of the newly made virus proteins set to work on. They soon have the cell churning out dozens of new snake-like strings of RNA. Some of those new RNA molecules contain the full set of genes, which will be packed inside new viruses. But what are the smaller ones doing?

Hang on, it looks like quite a lot of those new, small RNA molecules are moving off and finding dozens of other ribosomes. Now they're commanding those ribosomes to make masses and masses of virus proteins too. After all, it's impossible to make new viruses without an awful lot of new spike, nucleocapsid, envelope and membrane proteins.

Blimey! The virus is transforming our throat cell before our very eyes. It's as if a crazed new boss has stormed into a factory and taken it over by force. Not only do they have radical new ideas about what this factory should make, their production targets are seriously ambitious too. Some of the

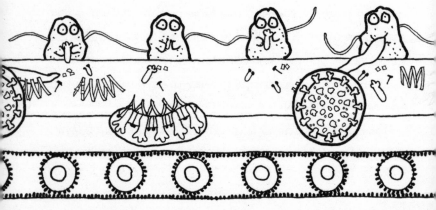

virus proteins are specifically designed to interfere with the cell's normal activities. They do this so effectively that the cell is soon working flat-out, devoting all its energy, raw materials and much of its protein workforce to the *virus's* plan.

The hijack is working so well that our throat cell basically stops everything it was doing before the virus barged in. Earlier today it was protecting the inside of the throat, and it's certainly not doing that any more. Now it's mass-producing proteins to build new viruses.

It's taken about 10 hours for the virus to infect and take control of our cell, and the first in a series of brand-spanking-new coronaviruses are just appearing. Each one is identical to the virus that infected the cell in the first place. Over the next 12 hours or so, row after row of viruses assemble before us – each a ghastly ball, bristling with those sinister spikes.

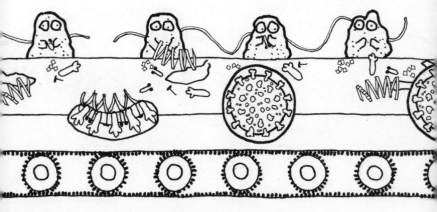

The cell has even wrapped all those new viruses up for delivery: each one is covered in an extra bubble of lipid membrane. Now the cell is sending all this deadly cargo to its outside edge, where the delivery bubbles fuse with the cell's outer membrane, releasing all those new viruses out into the world . . .

Oh, just look at my beautiful babies!
Now do you get my plan?

Huh? They don't look too cute to me.

Nooo! We'd better get out of here! Our throat cell looks like it's had enough. As far as we know, not all cells die immediately after being infected with the coronavirus, but some of them do. And this one definitely looks like it's fading fast. It's starting to dissolve – from the inside, which is where we are! We don't want to get dissolved too. Reverse the shrinking machine, quick!

Pheweee . . . that was hectic.

We saw some crazy stuff in there. *One* little virus forced its way into our throat cell and, over the course of 24 hours, it bossed that cell around to produce *one thousand* more viruses. Even rabbits can't breed that fast.

And just think . . . every single one of those thousand new

viruses could drift off and find another cell to ambush. Or get coughed out of one person's body and breathed in to someone else's. And then all those viruses can infect other cells and do the same thing . . . again . . . and again . . . and again . . .

Not bad for a day's work, eh?

Oh dear. Looks like this could get messy.

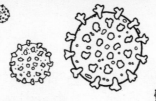

Chapter Three

Viruses on the Rampage

How they can rip through our bodies like a wildfire

A virus out in the open on its own is a pretty forlorn little package. It can't really do anything for itself, other than hang around hoping to find its way inside someone so it can infect them. But once it gets inside it springs into action, and uses our cells to reproduce itself with frightening efficiency. From that moment on, we humans are often playing catch-up. Before long, it's not just the workings of individual cells that the virus can reach into and hijack, but also whole organs or even entire bodies.

To see how viruses can do that, let's start by looking at how human populations grow, compared to the breakneck, burned-rubber pace at which viruses can reproduce.

If every pair of human parents have two children, they basically replace themselves in the next generation. If every couple had four children, the next generation would be double the size. Scientists say the *growth rate* of the population is **one** in the first example – because the second generation is the same size as the first. It's **two** in the second example, because there are twice as many children as parents.

We still don't know exactly how many new viruses the COVID-19 virus tends to make with each generation, but we do know that other fairly similar coronaviruses produce as many as a thousand viruses from each cell they infect. That means each generation could be one thousand times larger than the last! So we'd say the *growth rate* of those viruses would be **1,000**.

When populations – of humans, viruses or anything else – grow like this, with each generation multiplying the number found in the one before, it is called *exponential growth*. When the growth rate is high, as it is for many viruses, it can lead to changes that are both explosively fast and eye-wateringly massive.

To see quite how much difference the growth rate makes, imagine a village has a population of 100 people. They form 50 couples, and each couple has four children in each generation. So the growth rate is two. Here's how that population changes over four generations (assuming no one dies or moves away):

PEOPLE
Growth rate 2

100

300

700

1,500

3,100

Initial population

VIRUSES
Growth rate 1000

100

100

GENERATION 1

100 thousand
= a large town

GENERATION 2

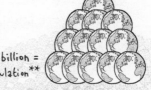

100 million =
1.5 × UK population*

GENERATION 3

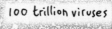

100 billion =
13 × Earth's population**

GENERATION 4

100 trillion viruses

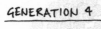

* UK Pop. over 67 million

** Earth Pop. 7.8 billion and growing

Quite different, isn't it?

Heck, after just *one* round of reproduction, the virus population was already the size of a large human town. And then in the next generation there were 1.5 times more viruses than there are people in the whole of the UK! And when *they* reproduced, there were suddenly 13 times more viruses than there are *people on the planet.* And after that the numbers just get silly: we end up with 100 trillion viruses.

To understand mega-numbers like that, it's helpful to look at the cells in the human body: the average adult is made from 37 trillion of them. That means that after just four rounds of reproduction a virus could have made enough new viruses to infect – and potentially kill – every single cell in the body. Not just once, but nearly three times over.

And it's not only that viruses can reach truly massive numbers in a few generations, they can also do it very quickly. If each human generation takes around 30 years, it would have taken 120 years for our imaginary population of 100 to reach 3,100. An individual coronavirus, on the other hand, can potentially produce a new generation of 1,000 viruses every 24 hours. Its population can rocket and, as our example showed, go stratospheric in just four days.

Starting to see now how a tiny, flea-sized virus could infest and overwhelm a sky-high giant?

Good! Now you're beginning to understand why they call me Coronavirus the Mighty. Run while you still can! And please stop comparing me to a flea...

No, you stop it. You're letting those big numbers go to your head.

And anyway, that 100 trillion number was just an example. In reality, a coronavirus infection can't grow and overwhelm a human body *quite so* quickly. Not every infected cell will follow the virus's instructions absolutely and produce 1,000 new viruses – especially once the body and the cell itself activates its antiviral defensive systems. And not every new virus will find a cell to infect. Partly, that's because your lungs and airways are lined with a thin layer of protective mucus, which can stop germs getting at cells. But it's also because the new coronavirus can only infect cells that have the ACE2 'lock' (see p. 23) at their surface. And, luckily for us, it's not on all of our cells.

Once the virus does find a way in and starts to multiply, it causes the COVID-19 illness. To understand this better we'll break it down into three phases. It's important to remember that most people get better after going through the first or the second phase, and only a minority of people experience the life-threatening third phase of the disease.

Phase 1: The stealthy incubation period

Most viral illnesses start gradually and quietly, and COVID-19 is no exception. For some viruses this *incubation period* is short. After you catch flu, you usually start to feel grotty about two days later. Other viruses take their time: the average incubation period for glandular fever (caused by the Epstein-Barr virus) is around a month. COVID-19 normally takes about five days to rear its ugly head, although sometimes the incubation period lasts 14 days or more.

But strange as it might seem, virus infections can be quite well advanced, with thousands or even millions of cells infected and damaged, and you still won't have any clue you've even got it growing inside your body. And actually, quite a lot of the people infected with the virus that causes COVID-19 hardly seem to feel ill at all. Scientists sometimes call them 'invisible' carriers of the virus. Thankfully, this seems to include most children. Plenty of children do catch it, but often they hardly suffer much more than the symptoms of a mild cold.

It's still not clear why lots of people get away with just a very mild dose of COVID-19. Perhaps it's partly to do with the way their immune systems keep it at bay. But it's also important to remember that the surfaces of our airways and lungs – the COVID-19 virus's favourite places to infect – cover a massive area.

Our lungs contain huge numbers of air-filled channels and pockets, a bit like a sponge, and they're all made from cells. Don't try this at home, but if you could somehow spread all the inner surface of an adult's lungs out flat, it'd be big enough to cover half a tennis court! What that means is that coronaviruses can infect and damage a lot of your cells and the chances are you won't feel a thing, because you have plenty more cells working just fine.

If my lungs are that big, why am I so out of breath?

Phase 2: Now it's getting nasty

One of the first and most common signs that COVID-19 could move on to the more serious second phase often seems

43

innocent enough: a dry, tickly cough. But what's actually going on inside the body is that the virus has done enough damage for us to start taking notice. If it kills enough cells in the lining of the nose, throat, trachea and lungs, it begins to literally tickle the ends of the nerve cells. It's those irritated nerves that make us cough.

At first, the body doesn't mind: coughing is our natural way of getting things out of the lungs and airways that shouldn't be there. And the virus definitely doesn't care – every cough is a chance for myriad virus particles to whirl off into the outside world and perhaps find a whole new giant human to infect.

But if the number of viruses keeps growing exponentially, the damage gets worse and the virus spreads deeper into the lungs. The cough can get much more painful and impossible to control. For some reason – nobody is quite sure what the virus is up to here – quite a few people lose their sense of smell and taste too. More often, people also have a high fever and generally feel tired, achy and unwell. That's why COVID-19 might seem a lot like a bad case of flu, but it's actually caused by a completely different virus.

> First you compared me to a flea, now to my distant cousin *influenza*. Whatever next? I am unique, I tell you.

You certainly are unique.

But nasty as Phase 2 can be, remember that most people do get better. It might take a couple of weeks of feeling truly rotten, or occasionally even longer, but they get through it. And while older people are more vulnerable, quite a few people aged over 100 years old have recovered from this illness.

For those who don't recover from Phase 2, things can get much worse.

Phase 3: Life in the balance

One of the biggest riddles still to be solved for this virus is why some people don't even notice they've got it, while others can quite suddenly develop an extremely severe disease. The risk of this happening is greater for some people than for others. That's why we need to do everything we can to make sure older people and people who already have health conditions, such as heart or lung problems, obesity or diabetes, don't catch it.

Phase 3 is the really risky phase. The one where the virus can eventually cause such havoc inside the lungs that they start filling up with fluid and the remains of viruses and dead cells. If this condition gets really bad it becomes hard, or even impossible, to breathe properly. This means the patient is suffering from pneumonia, which can stop them from absorbing enough oxygen into their blood. People who get to this point should be admitted to hospital immediately. Some will need to be connected to a ventilator, a machine that will help get that oxygen back into their bodies.

As viruses start to build up in massive numbers in the lungs and airways, they can get into the blood and hitch a ride to other parts of the body. Sometimes they affect the blood itself, by making it form dangerous clots, and the viruses can end up damaging the blood vessels, the heart, the kidneys, the liver, the intestines and perhaps even the brain. In all of these parts of the body there will be at least some cells that have the ACE2 lock, so the virus has a way to get in.

If it gets to this point, COVID-19 is very unpleasant and frightening, and extreme medical intervention has to be taken. Sometimes even that doesn't work and, sadly, not everyone gets better. There's still no cure for COVID-19, so even with the best treatment available, a small fraction of people infected by the virus will die.

It might sound strange, but some of the worst symptoms of viral illnesses aren't the effects of the virus itself. Sometimes the most serious effects of COVID-19, and also some of the milder symptoms, like the fever from Phase 2, are at least partly caused by the ways our bodies react to the infection.

But long before we feel any ill effects of the virus, the first stage of our body's reaction to it is when infected cells in the lungs and airways raise the alarm, dial 999, and summon the body's own emergency services.

Watch out, virus, here they come.

Oh snap. I don't like the sound of this one bit.

You'd better get ready, virus, because the immune system knows what it's up to.

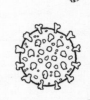

Chapter Four

Action Stations!

Meet your body's incredible homegrown emergency services

Standing in the way of the virus is one of the most wonderful things in the known universe: your immune system. However old you are, you can be one hundred per cent certain that your immune system has already saved your life – many, many times. And if you are unlucky enough to get infected with the COVID-19 virus, chances are your immune system will do it again. You probably won't even stop to thank it. But you should.

In fact, your incredible immune system isn't really a single thing at all. It's actually made of hundreds of billions of individual cells. These are your body's white blood cells. They have amazing powers that allow them to swallow, destroy or disable invading germs. They come in a huge variety of shapes and sizes and they're spread through almost all the different tissues and organs in your body.

Your immune system has no central brain to control it but, amazingly, all these different cells work together, like the parts of a well-oiled machine. And although your immune system has no eyes to see with, it keeps a constant watch

over your entire body. And when it detects damage, danger or something that just doesn't seem quite right, the whole system leaps into action.

You should see what goes on under your skin when you get an infection. It's spectacular! Countless thousands of different immune cells swarm through your body, like huge squadrons of highly trained police, fire and ambulance crews rushing to the scene of a major crime, accident or natural disaster. They've got a good few comic-book superheroes backing them up too.

As they move around the body, these different immune system cells are constantly chatting with each other using their own language of chemical signals. The most important of these chemicals are protein molecules called *cytokines*.

Your body makes more than 30 different cytokines, and they each give immune cells specific instructions. Some act at short range – only cells nearby can hear their commands. Others broadcast their message far and wide, often travelling through your bloodstream, telling other cells about a new threat, calling for reinforcements or suggesting a change of tactic.

This constant chemical chatter allows the different cells of the immune system to work out between themselves how they should respond to a particular wound or infection.

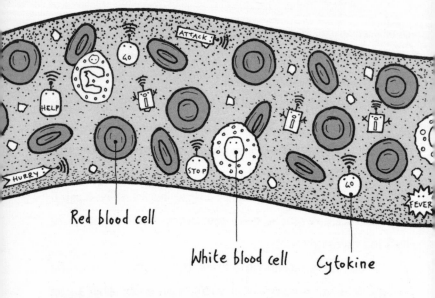

Red blood cell

White blood cell   Cytokine

Together, they have to decide whether something unfamiliar is a friend – like that nutritious cheese and pickle sandwich you just ate. Or a potential foe – like the germs lurking in the mouldy bit you didn't spot on one corner of that same sandwich. Then, once they decide there is a problem, the immune cells work out how best to deal with it.

It takes a lot of energy to run your immune system, so quite understandably your body doesn't want to draw on its great power more than it has to. That means it does what it can to keep viruses and other germs out of the body in the first place.

Most of the time all these different physical defences work

To tiny microbes your skin is as thick as reinforced concrete

Snot traps dirt and bugs like glue

A thin layer of snot-like mucus protects lungs and gut

Little hairs called cilia push the mucus and everything it traps away from your lungs

Spit, tears and stomach acid are like anti-germ potions

pretty well. But they don't always succeed.

Cut on your finger? Bacteria infecting your ear? Mouldy sandwich overwhelming your intestines? Or the COVID-19 virus getting through the mucus and infecting the cells in your throat? Whatever the problem, your immune system will quickly start figuring out its response.

It's still too early to know exactly how our bodies react

to the COVID-19 virus, and not everyone's immune system acts in the same way, but generally it responds to any harmful virus by unleashing three main waves of activity, each with its own specialized teams of highly skilled emergency service personnel.

Wave 1: The rapid-response units

Most of the cells in your body have ways of noticing that they've got a virus inside them. One way they respond is by releasing those cytokine messages, especially one called *interferon*.

Interferon is a warning message, alerting neighbouring cells that there's a dangerous virus on the loose. Then, as its name suggests, it *interferes*, with the virus's ability to get inside the body's cells and reproduce itself.

But interferon is also a distress signal. It sends an SOS

message to the brain and triggers a rise in temperature – that fever we heard about in Chapter 3. The fever is partly the body's way of telling you: 'You're sick, rest up'. But it's also an attempt to bake the virus, before it bakes you. Viruses and many other germs can't cope with the heat – it slows them down.

Within hours of your body detecting the virus, more blood starts flowing to the infected area – another effect triggered by fever and interferon – and immune cells start arriving.

First to the crime scene are the kind of law-enforcement officers who seize their suspects first and ask questions later.

They realize that something's up and leap straight in. Some of these cells are called *phagocytes*. These are cells with seriously big appetites. They engulf, gobble up and digest viruses, the remains of dead cells and even virus-infected cells – whole.

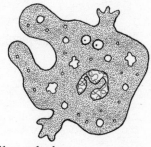

Neutrophils are also on the phagocyte's team, but as well as

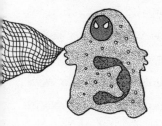

swallowing invaders, they have extra superpowers. Like Spider-Man, they shoot out a net, made of a mixture of protein and DNA fibres, to entangle germs and then reel them in and destroy them.

Then there are the *natural killer* cells. Really, the name says it all. If you were a cell, you wouldn't want to meet one of these guys on a dark night. When they get wind of an infection,

they sidle up to infected cells and release a spray of chemicals that peppers the target cell with holes.

Not sure I want to meet them either...

None of this is pretty, and it might sound odd that one of the immune system's first reactions is to intentionally *kill* virus-infected cells. But, really, when you're up against a fast-moving threat like a virus, it pays to take some pretty drastic action.

But even with this hard-hitting approach, the Wave 1 law-enforcement officers usually can't stop the virus in its tracks completely. They need back-up.

Wave 2: The highly trained specialists

While the Wave 1 hit squads were wading in with their pretty brutal, heavy-handed tactics, there were some more stealthy operatives on the job too: these are the *dendritic cells* (the name means 'tree-like' because they're covered with little branches). They tend not to be heavily armed, but they're absolutely crucial for sharing vital intelligence and co-ordinating the immune response.

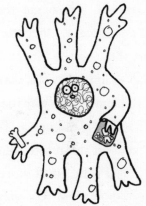

Dendritic cells are born in the marrow at the centre of your bones, but they leave home when they're very young and crawl out to every organ in your body. After they get there, they just hang out quietly, like spies operating undercover. They watch. And they listen . . .

And when dendritic cells notice something fishy, they come and investigate. What they really want is a piece of evidence they can use to brief other departments about what's going on in the current emergency. When they encounter a virus, they don't hang about. They swallow it, break it into pieces, then they immediately set off on another long journey through your body, carrying those bits of dead virus inside them.

They'll either be heading for an organ in your tummy called the spleen, or a lymph node (those lumps in your armpits, throat, groin, etc. that sometimes swell up when you're ill). These are the major training centres of the immune system. Once the dendritic cell sleuths get in, they start showing the bits of the virus they swallowed to other kinds of immune cells, particularly *T-cells* and *B-cells*.

Remember the way the virus's spike acted like a key (see p. 23)? Each individual T-cell and B-cell has a similar sort of 'key' on its surface. But now the 'lock' isn't the human ACE2, it's the bit of virus that the dendritic cell is holding out to show them. The immune system urgently wants to find T-cells and B-cells that have keys that fit the virus, because the cells that have the right match are the only ones that can instantly learn to sniff out, then snuff out, the virus.

The only trouble is, there are many billions of T-cells and B-cells in the body, and only very, very few of them hold the right key for this particular kind of virus. Imagine having a billion random keys and knowing only one of them will open your front door . . . that's what the immune system has to deal with. Luckily, however, the T-cells and B-cells file past the dendritic cells very, very quickly.

. . . Nope, Nope, Nope, Nope – Yesss!

As soon as a cell with the right key turns up, bingo! That cell gets an immediate promotion and prepares to be sent out on an assignment. But first it needs to build a team of identical operatives. All it has to do is reproduce itself by dividing one cell into two. And then have those two cells divide again, and so on, many times over. Within a couple of days, the chosen cell has built up a squad of hundreds or even thousands of identical clones (it's actually this build-up of cell numbers that can make your glands swell up and feel tender when you've got an infection). These T-cell and B-cell teams then move out and hitch a ride in the blood to the site of infection.

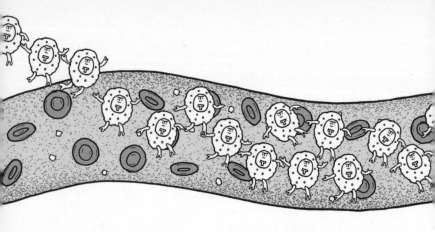

Once T-cells and B-cells have been activated, things get a bit more complicated, since they have several different ways of working. Let's take a closer look at some of them.

Killer T-cells: A bit like the natural killer cells from Wave 1, only they're not so trigger-happy. They use their 'key' to single out virus-infected cells and kill them without mercy.

> Come on ... this doesn't seem like a very fair game any more.

Well, it's not a game. And you started it, virus. These cells are just doing their job.

Helper T-cells: Crucial team players – they assess the situation and shout out helpful instructions to other kinds of immune cells when necessary. Among those they encourage are the big-mouthed phagocytes from Wave 1, who still have a lot more work to do, chomping up germs and infected cells.

One of the other vital things helper T-cells do is recruit and encourage more B-cells to join the action.

B-cells: Agents of the immune system that wield particularly powerful weapons called antibodies. These are molecules that use the same lock and key principle that you're

probably getting quite familiar with now. Each antibody 'key' matches a specific part of the virus. But rather than keeping them stuck to the outside of a cell, B-cells churn out these antibody keys in huge numbers – up to 2,000 identical antibodies every second – and release them into the blood.

So many antibodies are produced that it's only a matter of time before they bump into their matching 'lock' on the virus. When they hit that target, they latch on tight. Three things can happen next:

- When antibodies stick to a virus, they can stop it infecting other cells.
- They can glue lots of viruses together into a non-infectious clump: a ready meal for a phagocyte.
- They can act like a giant flag, with a message that reads 'Over here, immune system, come and get me!'

A good memory for bad germs

One of the most magnificent things about antibodies is the way our immune systems can remember how to make them, even long after we've recovered from illnesses. To do this, some of the B-cells become *memory cells*. (T-cells do this too, becoming memory T-cells). And – you guessed it – these cells are the main way the immune system remembers.

Once memory cells are made they can survive for several decades. And if they ever bump into the same germ again, they can start churning out the right antibodies and activate T-cells straight away. The first time we get an infection it usually takes several days to get the teams of Wave 2 immune cells going, but memory cells can whip them into action far more quickly. Often that's enough to stop an infection before it's even started.

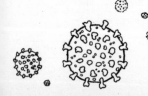

This kind of memory is called *immunity*. And it's very helpful indeed. After a viral infection like measles, for example, immunity usually lasts for the rest of someone's life: if you've had it, you never get it again. Against other viruses, including some of those that cause flu, immunity may only last for a few weeks or months. As for the COVID-19 virus, everyone desperately hopes immunity will last a long time, but it's still too early to know for sure. Based on the way people react to the other kinds of coronaviruses, most scientists think immunity to this one could last for between one and three years. Vaccines trigger immunity too – they make sure you get the protection, without having to first suffer from the illness itself.

Wave 3: The clear-up operation

We're coming to the final stages of the immune response to the virus and the key players now are the *regulatory T-cells*, or *T-regs* (pronounced like the dinosaur *T. rex* – but they're infinitesimally smaller and less dangerous). You can think of T-regs as part commanding officers, part firefighters and part community support officers.

The immune teams of Wave 1 and Wave 2 inflict quite a

lot of damage on the body's own cells. If that goes on for too long, it can cause serious problems. So it's up to the T-regs to judge when the job of fighting off the virus has been done and enough is enough. That's when they turn on the firehoses to take the heat out of the immune response and generally do what they can to restore calm to the situation.

It was a cytokine called interferon that raised the alarm and got the immune system all fired up. Now T-regs produce cytokines that work in the opposite way – they order many of the other immune cells to stop their attacks.

TIDYING UP THE MESS

We're near the end of the infection and many of those immune cells have been working away without rest for days. When they're told to stop they just collapse, as if they're exhausted, and die! The pus that builds up in infected wounds is mostly made up of dead immune cells. Similar stuff can build up in the lungs in serious cases of COVID-19.

T-regs don't just order immune cells to stop working, though, they also put other cells to work; they bring some of the thuggish phagocytes from Wave 1 into line, setting them to work hoovering up the mess of dead cells and viruses. If all goes to plan, the three great waves of the immune system all work together to send the virus packing. But the immune system is always walking a tightrope, trying to find the right balance between stopping the virus and not hurting the body. And sadly it doesn't always work.

Many doctors think that some of the worst COVID-19 symptoms are triggered when the three waves fail to co-ordinate themselves properly. If Wave 3 can't get Waves 1 and 2 under control, the immune system can go into overdrive instead, sometimes launching fierce attacks on several of the body's internal organs at once – even the ones that aren't infected by the virus at all. This is called a *cytokine storm*, because it's caused by massive over-production of cytokines, which activates a storm of immune cells. They can cause blood pressure to drop and stop vital organs working properly. People can recover from this, but it's an extremely unpleasant experience for the person involved and everyone who cares for them.

Keep in mind that this only happens to a small fraction of patients. Far, far more more people get better than die from the virus. And that's all thanks to the extraordinary workings of our immune systems. In fact, immune responses are usually so effective they make mere survival a challenge for many viruses. If a virus infection wants to keep going, it can't just focus on spreading throughout one person's body, it's got to find a way to spread to other people too. And it often has to do that pretty sharpish, before our immune system finds it and obliterates it.

You don't need to tell me that.
This chapter's been horrific. I'm getting out of here!

I know. But I have funny feeling we're not quite shot of you yet . . .

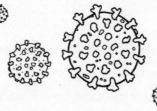

Chapter Five
Going Viral

How viruses leap from person to person and travel around the world

You've probably heard the expression 'going viral'? We use it to describe how crazes for new toys or hobbies spread through schools and across whole countries. Or how fashions, songs, weird hairstyles, online memes and videos of cats can be nowhere one minute and everywhere the next.

What these things have in common is that they can all build very quickly on their past successes. In other words, they can all spread by growing *exponentially*. And, as you probably remember from page 38, that is precisely what some viruses try to do once they get inside our bodies. It's part of their bid to spread through as many bodies as possible.

So if one of these viruses is to 'go viral' and spread across a whole city – or even across the world – it has a race to win. Its opponent is the immune system and the prize is survival. To keep an outbreak going, the virus has to make sure it can jump from one host to another before either:

a) the host's immune system kills or disables the virus, or

b) the virus completely incapacitates – or kills – its host.

(Scientists love using this word 'host' for the people or

creatures viruses infect, as if the virus is a welcome guest, which it most definitely isn't!)

These viruses can move pretty quickly, so if we don't want them to win, we have to do our best to keep one step ahead of them.

The COVID-19 virus that began causing such havoc around the world in 2020 shows quite how fast viruses can spread. So far as we know the first time this virus ever infected a human was in the Chinese city of Wuhan, in November 2019 (that's where the '19' comes from in COVID-19). By spring 2020 it had reached every continent (apart from Antarctica), leaving a trail of destruction behind it. To understand how the virus did that, we need to understand how it managed to get such a big head start over us.

Firstly, there's that 5–14 day incubation period (see p. 42), where the virus quietly builds up its numbers before making anyone feel ill. It turns out that before this period is even over, our bodies can start producing and releasing enough viruses to infect other people. So the people incubating the illness, we might call them 'incubators', can spread the virus for at least two days, or even longer, before showing any symptoms and without having any idea that the virus is working away inside their bodies.

Then there are the 'invisibles' – the people who seem to

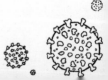

get the virus, and can pass it on, but never suffer much at all. Early in an outbreak, the 'incubators' and the 'invisibles' just get on with living their lives as usual. They go to school, college and work. Thousands of them hop on and off busy trains and buses; go to football matches, concerts and museums; and take flights between countries and between continents.

I don't care if I don't have any wings.
Just watch me fly.

We'll bring you back down to earth soon enough.

And the new coronavirus didn't just succeed in getting to every corner of the planet; it also knew exactly how to infect people along the way.

The COVID-19 virus can survive for several hours in the tiny droplets of water, snot or saliva that we expel when we cough, sneeze and maybe even breathe out. It can also lurk like a dangerous fingerprint in the invisible smears we leave on door handles, desks and train seats. Then, of course, it can get from these surfaces into our mouths and noses from our hands when we touch our faces.

Before long the virus was nearly everywhere and getting inside huge numbers of human bodies. But luckily for us, it isn't quite so skilled at hopping from person to person as it is from cell to cell. As we saw in Chapter 3, each infected cell has the potential to infect a thousand other cells. A single infected person can't spread it to anything like that number of other people.

Scientists think that, even in the early stages of an outbreak, when everyone is a potential target and people are mixing with each other as normal, each person with the COVID-19 virus infects on average two or three other people. That's *on average* – some people don't spread it to anyone else and others are 'super-spreaders' who, for reasons no one has worked out yet, seem able to infect lots more people.

One infection leading to two new infections might not sound too bad. But that still means the number of cases doubles with every round of infection; and that can still lead to exponential growth.

If you stepped out of your house and took 30 steps along the street you wouldn't travel all that far.

Now imagine you've got super-extending legs that mean each step you take is twice as long as the one before. If your first step was 0.5 metres long, your second would be one metre, your third two metres and so on . . . all quite manageable.

But your 15th step would be a 16 km leap out of your neighbourhood . . .

Believe it or not, your 27th step would take you looping one and a half times round the whole world (those magic legs would have to be mind-bogglingly extendable).

And when it comes to the new coronavirus, it can clock up lots of generations of doubling pretty quickly. When allowed to spread through a group of people that haven't had it before, scientists think the total number of infections can double, on average, every six or seven days. And as happened with your steps, the spread of the virus won't seem so dramatic at first. Then BOOM, suddenly it's everywhere.

That's precisely what happened with COVID-19. For quite some time after the first case was confirmed on 17 November 2019, the disease seemed mainly to affect one province in China. When a disease outbreak spreads like this in a single part of the world, it's known as an *epidemic*.

But then cases started cropping up in several other countries.

By 11 March 2020, the disease had shown up in 114 countries and was officially defined as a *pandemic*, which meant that *epidemics* had broken out almost everywhere in the world.

Then, on 2 April 2020, COVID-19 reached another unwelcome landmark: a total of one million known cases were confirmed worldwide. Going from one to a million cases took just over **19 weeks**. The second million known cases appeared just **two weeks** later*.

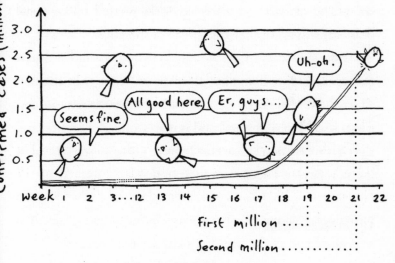

* Once people started changing their behaviour to slow the virus down, COVID-19 couldn't keep up this rate of exponential doubling.

73

You see, that's how I do it. There's no magic, just some pretty simple maths. A bit of exponential growth and some coughing humans and I can be anywhere I want.

Hmm, yes. You're even more of a threat than I thought. You don't just stop whole human giants, you can bring our whole world to a standstill . . .

Even if a disease only makes a small fraction of the people it infects seriously ill, and then only a fraction of those people die, when that disease is as fast-moving as COVID-19 the number of tragedies can quickly add up. This is why, during the spring of 2020, so many countries started taking some drastic measures to slow the spread of the virus.

There are lots of things we can do to outpace and outsmart this virus, and we'll find out about those in the next chapter. The trouble is, we're up against loads of other viruses too, and they use all kinds of weird and not-so-wonderful tactics, and they definitely don't play fair. If we're going to stay ahead of them, it pays to understand their tricks.

The dreaded spread

Some viruses spread by taking advantage of their host's normal bodily functions, as happens with the cough you

can get from COVID-19. Others let unsuspecting insects do the spreading for them. Some viruses are always in a hurry. Others take their time. Here are a few popular strategies that help diseases spread; you'll notice that some viruses sneakily use more than one technique.

1. Going airborne

Examples: COVID-19, flu, measles, smallpox, chickenpox and the common cold (caused by a range of different rhinoviruses, adenoviruses and coronaviruses)

Description: These viruses prefer to travel from person to person in tiny drops of snot and saliva. They can irritate our nerves and make us cough and sneeze, expelling viruses into the air we breathe.

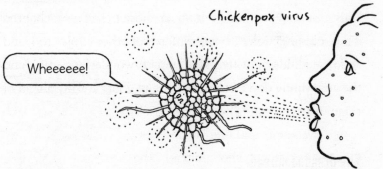

Shockingly: Measles is caused by one of the most infectious viruses known. An infected person can transmit the virus to nine out of every ten non-immune people they get close to.

Wow! Think of all I could achieve if I was as infectious as measles!

Luckily: COVID-19 definitely can't spread as easily as measles. There are also simple things that can help reduce the spread of all these viruses, like handwashing and coughing or sneezing into a tissue (then throwing the tissue away carefully).

2. Gut reactions

Examples: rotavirus, norovirus

Description: These viruses get in through our mouths and infect and kill the cells that line our guts. This can stop our bodies from absorbing fluids, causing violent bouts of diarrhoea and projectile vomiting. Nice! And for the very young or very frail, prolonged diarrhoea can be a killer.

Give me a hand!

Norovirus

It's the vomit and diarrhoea these illnesses produce that spread the disease. They're packed with viruses: up to 30 billion per teaspoonful, although it only takes ten to start an infection. They can also survive for weeks outside the body, travelling from toilet seats and taps to hands and into people's stomachs.

Shockingly: Viruses that cause diarrhoea kill more than a quarter of a million children aged under five each year, mainly in poorer countries.

Luckily: These viruses can be fairly easily beaten, so long as we can make sure everyone in the world has access to clean water, working toilets and any available vaccines.

3. The touchy-feely approach

Examples: smallpox, chickenpox, Ebola, glandular fever, warts, verrucas and cold sores, and all the other airborne and gut-loving viruses in (1) and (2)

Description: 'Touchy-feely' definitely doesn't mean 'friendly' here. Smallpox was one of the nastiest, most lethal diseases there's ever been. It made people's skin erupt in painful fluid-filled blisters that teemed with viruses. When the blisters popped and scabbed over, sufferers would spread the infection to anyone, and on to anything, they touched. Thank goodness it's no longer a threat, thanks to a global vaccination programme. Chickenpox isn't as nasty, but it spreads in a similar way. Warts and verrucas can survive on surfaces infected people have touched, but they like it

Ebola virus

best when we touch each other directly. As does Ebola, one of the few viruses that can be as deadly as smallpox. Cold sores and glandular fever spread best when we kiss.

Waiting for people to kiss is just plain lazy!

Shockingly: Ebola is one of the most horribly lethal viruses ever. During the first known outbreak in the Democratic Republic of Congo in 1976 nearly 90% of victims died.
Luckily: The first vaccine was approved in 2019.

4. Mixing of bodily fluids
Examples: hepatitis B, hepatitis C, HIV-1
Description: For some viruses, touch on its own isn't enough. They need a mixing of people's blood or other bodily fluids in order to spread. Hepatitis B can damage the liver and sometimes even cause liver cancer. It can be transmitted if several people are injected with the same unsterilized needle, or when people have sex, or from mother to baby during birth, for example. HIV-1, the virus that causes the disease AIDS (acquired immune deficiency syndrome), spreads in a

similar way. Deviously, it tries to avoid the immune system by infecting and destroying some of the white blood cells most needed to fight it off.

Shockingly: Since HIV-1 was identified in the 1980s, it has infected 75 million people and killed around 32 million.

Luckily: Scientists have invented good drug treatments for AIDS, although they're expensive and not always easy to get hold of, especially for people in poorer countries.

5. The sneaky, persistent method

Examples: chickenpox, HIV-1, glandular fever, warts, verrucas and cold sores

Description: Did you spot the overlap with categories (3) and (4) above? It's no coincidence. Some viruses can lie low and bide their time until there's a chance to jump to another host.

Viruses that cause warts, verrucas, cold sores and glandular fever can lie dormant in a person but flare up again when they're ill or stressed. And, after we've recovered from chickenpox, our bodies never get rid of the virus altogether. Instead, it just hangs out quietly inside some of our nerve cells. Decades later it can wake up again, and cause an illness called shingles. And

I can wait.

Glandular fever virus

once you've got shingles, you can infect other people with chickenpox all over again.

Shockingly: HIV-1 doesn't just lie low, it mixes its genes with the human genes of the cells it infects. From that moment on the virus's genes are essentially part of the cell. So wherever the infected cell goes, and whatever it does, the HIV-1 genes go too.

What, it actually becomes part of a human cell?

Yup! It's a mean trick that makes it much harder to get rid of. Good job you can't do that.

6. *Hitching a ride in a bug*

Examples: yellow fever, dengue fever, Zika fever, chikungunya and Rift Valley fever are all carried by mosquitoes. Bourbon virus, Heartland virus and tick-borne encephalitis prefer to go by tick. Phlebotomus fever travels by sandfly.

Description: This is an effective strategy for viruses that like to infect a variety of animals. Mosquitoes and ticks don't mind too much where their blood meals come from: cow, horse, bird, monkey or human, who cares? And these freeloading viruses don't just get a ride between hosts; when the virus-carrying bugs bite us, they also inject their invisible passengers directly, and itchily, through our skin and into our bodies.

Shockingly: Mosquitoes breed where it's warm, rainy and humid. If they start to flourish in new places as the climate crisis makes the planet warmer, the viruses they carry will flourish too.

Luckily: Scientists are developing ways to stop

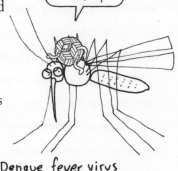

Dengue fever virus

mosquitoes spreading disease, by deliberately infecting them with certain bacteria or tinkering with their genes. While we wait to see if that works, keep applying that insect repellent.

Bonus Fact: Malaria is probably the best known, most lethal insect-borne disease, but it's not a virus; it's caused by tiny single-celled life forms called plasmodia.

7. Hacking our brains

Examples: rabies

Description: The rabies virus doesn't leave too much to chance. It's transmitted via the saliva of infected animals, which is why you really don't want to be bitten by a rabid dog (or a rabid bat, fox, wolf, monkey, cat, raccoon, etc.). Once the rabies virus is inside a body, it makes its way into nerve fibres and starts heading straight for the brain.

Once it's inside the brain, the worst of the symptoms start, and the infection is almost always lethal. So that's when the virus's race for survival really kicks in. It needs to get out of its current host and find a new host fast. So it does all it can to make its victims lose all sense of fear and become hyperactive and highly aggressive. Before long they are likely to be rushing around attacking other creatures. If that sounds like a nightmare, basically, it is.

Shockingly: That's not all. Rabies can also make those it infects terribly afraid of water, and turns swallowing into an agonizing ordeal. It causes the victim's mouths to overflow with highly infectious saliva – before they start biting.

Luckily: There's an effective vaccine for rabies. And it doesn't just stop people getting the disease, so long as it's given fairly soon after someone's been bitten, it can stop the virus too.

Now that really is one sick virus. Even I'm shocked by the way rabies behaves.

Zombie caterpillars

Rabies is bad, but what the baculovirus does to the gypsy moth caterpillar is worse. First, it flicks some hidden switch in the caterpillar's brain that makes it climb up into the treetops. Then the virus goes on a killing spree, turning the caterpillar into a sack of liquefied goo; its skin splits open and globs of highly infectious, virus-filled caterpillar slurry start raining down onto the leaves below, infecting other unsuspecting caterpillars. It's like the worst zombie movie ever. And, of course, the poor gypsy moth caterpillar dies.

Must. Climb. Tree . . .

Scary as these tricksy and sometimes downright manipulative virus tactics seem, you'll be relieved to know there's still a long way to go in this race. And we don't just have to rely on our fantastic immune systems: unlike viruses, humans know how to get ahead by working as a team. And because of that, we can do SCIENCE.

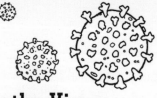

Chapter Six
Science vs the Virus
How we can stay one step ahead

For as long as people have been on this planet, we've had to put up with viruses that choose us as their hosts.

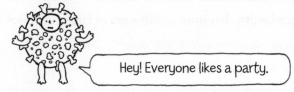

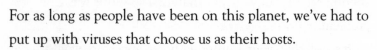

Hey! Everyone likes a party.

Yes, but nobody likes gatecrashers like you.

The first modern humans (*Homo sapiens*) evolved about 200,000 years ago, roughly 195,000 years before the first pyramid was built in ancient Egypt. We call this time prehistory. It was a long period, when most people lived in small tribes or family groups, roaming their local neighbourhoods, hunting, gathering and generally scavenging for a living.

At first, they probably didn't have to worry *too* much about viruses, because many of the viruses that cause the worst outbreaks (and the biggest problems) simply love crowds. In crowded places, it's much easier for them to spread. And since our immune systems usually do a pretty good job of quashing the viruses that cause illnesses like flu, measles and common colds, these crowd-loving viruses need to make sure they can jump to their next host before their first host recovers.

But back in prehistory, there weren't all that many humans about, and for many crowd-loving viruses, this was a bit of a problem.

It's not that your hunter-gatherer ancestors would have been in perfect health. Far from it. All sorts of bacteria, fungi and other parasites would have caused them all manner of problems. Nor would they have been virus-free. Nasty viral diseases like rabies would almost certainly have taken their toll from time to time, but without big populations, major epidemics were probably rare.

Many scientists think the human viruses that thrived best in those days were probably the sneaky, persistent ones, particularly the milder varieties. We can usually live quite happily with a few cold sores, warts and verrucas. From the virus's point of view, if their host doesn't bump into lots of other people very often, it's not a smart tactic to kill them off, or even confine them to bed, too quickly.

Around 12,000 years ago, some bright sparks who lived in the part of the world now known as the Middle East, decided to stop wandering so much and, quite literally, put down roots. They began farming, growing seasonal crops such as wheat, barley and peas. Then they started taming animals and keeping them for food, transport and company. Not having to search for food constantly made life much easier, in some ways.

Villages sprang up, then towns, then cities. Eventually whole empires were formed, crisscrossed by roads and connected together by seafaring ships. Now people were bumping into each other much more often, as they travelled on the roads and ships, and as people gathered and mingled in the villages, towns and ports.

Meanwhile, viruses that for millions of years had been living quite successfully in herds of non-human animals, suddenly started to move too. Cows, horses, pigs, goats and sheep were some of the first animals our ancestors decided to tame and breed. They gave our ancestors meat and dairy, helped pull ploughs and carry heavy loads. Over the centuries, they've been very generous with their viruses too.

Wash your hams.

Thanks to all these invited animal guests, and with a few donations from the rats, mice and insects that flocked into our ancestors' homes uninvited, we got a whole new crop of viruses. These included measles, mumps, influenza, rotaviruses and smallpox, not to mention a nasty selection of non-viral diseases too.

Viruses made a big impression on humanity's early civilizations:

- The distinctive scars caused by smallpox can be seen on the faces of 3,000-year-old Egyptian mummies.
- Some Egyptian paintings show people who've been affected by polio, a viral illness that can partially paralyse some of its victims.
- There's even evidence that, 2,500 years ago, ancient Greeks suffered painful swollen glands and cheeks caused by mumps.

The long and the short of it was, epidemics started breaking out and spreading further and faster than ever before, and, without cures, the best most people could do was hope and pray.

It took thousands of years, but eventually, thank goodness, modern science began to take shape, starting around 500 years ago. In time, it would bring more effective remedies, but progress in tackling viruses was still painfully slow. The first microscope was invented over 400 years ago, in 1590, but to actually see viruses we had to wait until 1931, when more powerful electron microscopes were invented. Before then no one knew what they looked like, and they barely had any clue how they worked.

And we've still got a huge amount to learn about viruses today, which is why the COVID-19 virus surprised almost everyone and triggered such pandemonium in 2020. It was a new virus that behaved in new and often unpredictable ways.

But at least scientists and doctors know *how* to go about cracking a new virus's mysteries. They might start asking impossible-sounding questions like, 'How can we make sure no one gets infected with this virus ever again?' Finding the answers could take them years or even decades, but they'll always learn new and useful things along the way.

Our knowledge of viruses – and what to do about the ones that harm us – is getting a bit better every single day. And that means there are masses of things that science can do to help humans stay one step ahead of the viruses. First, we can try . . .

Stopping the spread
Lockdown medieval-style

People weren't completely clueless about how diseases spread in the past. In medieval times, if someone noticed a neighbour was vomiting, feverish and had black pustules on their skin, they'd be just as likely to keep their distance as you would today.

By the way, those were symptoms of an actual disease that started rampaging around the world in the 1340s. It was known as the Black Death*, and infected people often died just three days after those symptoms began to show.

> Wow! The Black Death! I've heard about that. Didn't it kill one third of all humans in a single pandemic ...?

Don't get any ideas, virus, there's no way you could bring about anything like that much destruction. And anyway the Black Death was caused by bacteria; it wasn't one of your lot.

When the Black Death swept through medieval Europe, anyone who saw a building marked with a red cross knew to stay away. Houses were sometimes boarded up, even when residents were only *suspected* of having the disease. Whole

---

* We now call the disease bubonic plague. Even today it occasionally resurfaces and causes small outbreaks, but nowadays we can treat it with antibiotics.

villages could be sealed off to stop the disease spreading.

This was basically 'social distancing' and 'lockdown' medieval-style – scientists recommended similar measures to governments in many parts of the world in 2020.

Social distancing just means 'don't get too close to people who might be infected' and lockdown means 'stay at home'. Today we know 'self-isolation' is crucial too. That's when an infected person stays away from everyone else, as soon as they realize they've got the virus, until they're no longer infectious. Together, these measures can definitely slow the spread of a disease and stop hospitals getting overwhelmed. The aim is to ensure each infected person spreads the virus, on average, to less than one other person. When that happens, the epidemic's growth rate (see p. 38) becomes negative and it starts to fade away.

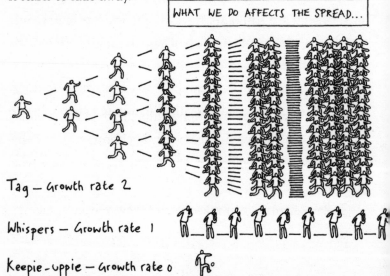

WHAT WE DO AFFECTS THE SPREAD...

Tag – Growth rate 2

Whispers – Growth rate 1

Keepie-uppie – Growth rate 0

Lockdown works, but it's tough for people of all ages. And ideally we'd only need them in the most extreme cases. If we can work out exactly how a virus spreads, it should be possible to slow transmission by making more precise changes to our lives. For example, if a virus travels through the air we can:

- do experiments to check whether wearing a face mask can stop it

- work out whether it's enough to stay a metre away from infected people – or if we really do need to keep a wall between us and the virus

- find out who the super-spreaders are (see p. 70) and encourage them to lie low.

In medieval times people had no hope of knowing the answers to these questions, so it's easy to see why running a mile, or barricading others into their homes and villages made sense. We still don't have all the answers, but, thanks to science, we do at least know where to look.

Testing, testing

Until very recently, it was often so difficult to make a definite diagnosis of many viral diseases that patients usually either died or recovered before doctors could know for sure what had made them ill.

Today scientists can take a small sample from someone's

body – in the case of COVID-19 it's a swab from their throat or some saliva – and test it to find out whether a virus is present. These tests often use chemical reactions to detect a virus's genes. Just as different foods in a supermarket have specific barcodes, every strain of virus has its own unique set of genes, made from either RNA or DNA, which can be clearly identified through testing.

Once doctors know which virus is making their patient ill they can make much better decisions about how to treat them.

Often gene tests can detect a virus in someone's body before they've even started feeling poorly. That can be fantastically helpful for an illness like COVID-19, because if the 'invisibles' and the 'incubators' (see pp. 68-9) can be identified, they can be asked to steer clear of other people until their infectious period is over.

Hey, that's not fair. I thought I was operating under the radar here.

Not so, virus; you may be invisible, but we're developing all kinds of different ways to see you.

We can use information from tests like this to stop anyone who works close to other people – especially nurses, doctors and care workers – from spreading the disease. In spring 2020, it was estimated that up to one fifth of hospital patients who suffered COVID-19 in the UK caught the virus when they were in hospital for something else.

Some tests can even show if you've already had an infection, by checking your blood for the kind of antibodies (see p. 61) that target a particular virus. If the right antibodies show up, it means your immune system has already fought the virus off, or is still sorting out the invaders.

Virus tests are getting more reliable and more sensitive all the time. They're also getting more inventive. For example, researchers are hoping to train dogs to sniff out infected people. And – hold your nose – it seems people with

COVID-19 can pass out fragments of the COVID-19 virus's genes in their poo. That means sampling the waste in a town's sewage works for virus genes could be an accurate way to see how many people are carrying the virus. One day it might even be possible for your toothbrush to automatically detect any unwanted germs inside your body and alert you and your doctor immediately!

That invention may be way off in the future, but today scientists called epidemiologists use the statistics from virus tests to make complex calculations that can help us predict:

- how many people are likely to get a virus
- where they're most likely to get it, and
- who they're most likely to catch it from.

Like weather forecasts, *virus* forecasts aren't always perfect, but they're definitely helpful, especially for governments that are trying to make decisions about things like reopening shops and cafés and letting people go back to school or work.

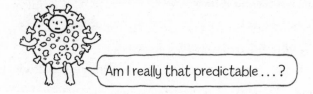

Am I really that predictable ... ?

You definitely surprised us at first. But now we're figuring out your little tricks.

Washing viruses down the plughole

Nooo, this is the bit about soap, isn't it?

Yup.

Does it seem as if you're constantly being nagged (even by politicians and newsreaders) to 'wash your hands . . . properly . . . with soap!'?

It probably doesn't feel like it, but they're actually doing you a favour, because when it comes to doing away with coronaviruses, plain old soap actually beats hand sanitizers and antibacterial wipes any day.

Because soap molecules are similar in shape to the lipid molecules in the virus's membrane envelope, they can wheedle their way in amongst those lipids and literally dissolve the virus's shell. For the same reason, soap also does a good job of detaching viruses from your hands. But at a microscopic level your skin is extremely rough and wrinkly and there are lots of nooks and crannies for viruses to hide in, which is why it's so important to rub away for a full 20 seconds.

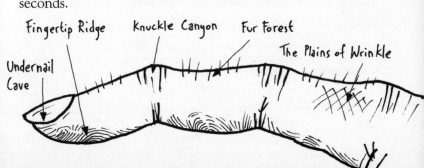

Fingertip Ridge   Knuckle Canyon   Fur Forest

The Plains of Wrinkle

Undernail Cave

You might find it hard to believe, but handwashing has most likely saved more lives than any other invention in all of history.

Dr Ignaz Semmelweis was the first person to truly understand the importance of handwashing as a way to prevent diseases spreading. He worked on a maternity ward in Austria in the 1840s and was alarmed by the number of young mothers in his care who caught nasty infections and died. But he also noticed that some of his doctor colleagues didn't clean their hands between handling dead bodies and delivering babies*. He set about persuading them to try washing their hands properly to see if it made a difference.

The effects were miraculous. The number of deaths on his ward plummeted almost instantly, and eventually Semmelweis's breakthrough led scientists to understand that most infectious diseases are caused by microscopic pathogens – viruses and bacteria. Since then, through encouraging people to wash their hands regularly, Semmelweis's discovery has probably helped to save millions, or even billions, of lives.

And here's an experiment carried out in the 1960s that shows why regularly washing your hands with soap is so crucial when we're up against highly infectious viruses, like

---

*Mothers whose babies were delivered by midwives were safe, because the midwives weren't touching dead bodies.

the ones that cause COVID-19, flu, diarrhoea and even the common cold.

A group of British scientists set out to understand how cold viruses spread. They invented a small contraption that slowly trickled liquid from the nose of one of the researchers – just as our noses can drip liquid snot when we've got a cold. But instead of invisible viruses, the fake snot contained an invisible dye that only shows up under ultraviolet (UV) light.

The researchers then invited a bunch of volunteers into the lab to play cards. After the game, they switched the lights off and turned a UV light on. They were astonished when they saw where the dye-laced 'snot' had got to. In less than an hour, it had spread nearly everywhere! It wasn't just on the cards and the table, it showed up on the fingers and faces of all the unsuspecting volunteers, on light switches, door handles and beyond.

We all touch our faces about 20 to 30 times every hour, without even realizing it. That's why, if we're not careful, viruses can get into our bodies so easily and spread from person to person.

Sadly we can't prevent any pandemic with soap alone. With a highly infectious virus, some people will always get ill, and then you've got to hope that doctors know how to treat the disease.

Stopping the symptoms

If your throat, your ear or any other part of your body gets badly infected by bacteria, your doctor can usually prescribe a course of antibiotics to cure it. Most of the time these medicines work brilliantly, attacking the bacteria and hardly doing any harm to your body's own cells.

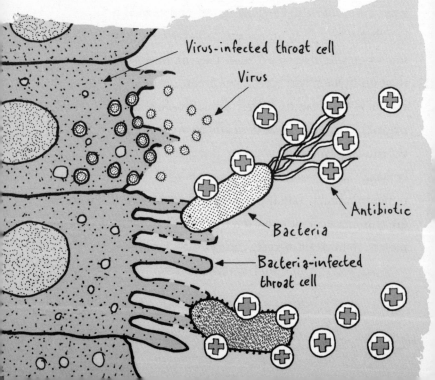

Virus-infected throat cell

Virus

Antibiotic

Bacteria

Bacteria-infected throat cell

Making medicines that work as well against viruses is harder, partly because viruses and bacteria operate very differently. Viruses are smaller and less complicated than bacteria, so there's not much for medicines to attack. And because viruses mainly work by hijacking our cells, antiviral medicines might rid us of the virus, but mess up our otherwise healthy cells.

This can be quite a challenge, but scientists have had a few spectacular successes. Not so long ago AIDS was always a fatal disease. Today potent medicines called anti-retrovirals can stop HIV-1, the virus that causes AIDS, in its tracks. As a result millions of people can live long and perfectly healthy lives, even with the virus inside their body.

We don't have a cure for the COVID-19 illness yet. But as soon as it was discovered, scientists and doctors all over the world launched a massive effort to test thousands of different chemical compounds on the virus, to see if anything could stop it, or simply slow it down to prevent the most life-threatening symptoms.

Many scientists think we can also learn from the way the human immune system deals with the virus. Let's eavesdrop on this conversation between a doctor and a recovering patient to find out more . . .

Now you've recovered from COVID-19, your blood should be swarming with antibodies against the virus.

Ew, not sure I like the sound of that.

Actually, it's great. If we clean up your blood and clear out any leftover viruses, we could inject it into a patient who's struggling to recover.

I'd like to help another patient!

Well, in theory, donating your blood could help two or three other patients get better.

Ugh, I'm feeling really weak again. Isn't there any other way to get the antibodies?

Well, scientists are trying to make them, with the help of various animals. It turns out llamas can make antibodies called nanobodies that stop viruses infecting our cells. If all goes to plan, those friendly llamas could soon be churning out masses of virus-blocking antibodies to use as a COVID-19 medicine.

That's amazing!

Always happy to help!

Of course, it would be even more amazing if scientists could stop people getting sick in the first place.

Stopping the virus

In 1721 an epidemic of smallpox (see p. 77) broke out in England. As the dreadful virus did its dreadful work, a wealthy woman called Lady Mary Wortley Montagu offered some peculiar advice. She told people to *deliberately infect* their children with the virus! She'd seen it done in Turkey, then had her own children infected. Lady Mary even convinced King George I of England that his granddaughters – potential heirs to the throne – should have the treatment.

In fact, people in China and India had already been doing it for a thousand years by that point. The process is called *inoculation* and here's how it worked.

First they found someone with smallpox and stuck a needle into one of their virus-laden pustules. Next they used that same needle to scratch the skin of someone who hadn't had the disease.

Normally, the inoculation then caused a small infection on the skin, which would usually be enough to trigger a full immune response. The inoculated person ended up with memory B-cells that produced those crucial protective

101

antibodies, and gained immunity to smallpox for life! Hurray!

It was a slightly risky process, though. A small fraction of people ended up getting full-blown smallpox when they might never have caught it in the first place. Later in the eighteenth century, an English doctor called Edward Jenner found a safer way to inoculate patients by using a very similar virus; one that gives cows an infection called cowpox, but hardly troubles people at all.

Jenner also came up with the word 'vaccine'. It was his way of thanking the cows, because 'vaccinus' means 'from a cow' in Latin. It describes something we can put into our bodies that mimics an infection so effectively that our immune systems come rushing in to defend us from the new threat. What our immune systems don't know is that a well-designed vaccine can't actually do us much harm. A vaccine against a virus might be made from part of the virus, like the COVID-19 virus's spike, or it might be a severely weakened version of the whole virus. When all goes to plan, vaccines stimulate the formation of memory B-cells and T-cells, which give us long-lasting immunity to a pathogen without us having to suffer many, if any, of the symptoms of a real infection. Clever stuff!

In 1980, after a massive international effort to snuff out the last epidemics with vaccination and block the spread of the virus, the world declared victory over smallpox. The virus had been driven to extinction.

> That vaccine can't have killed off *every single* smallpox virus!

Yes it did. We wiped smallpox from the face of the Earth. And we'd happily do the same to you.

In truth, a few top-secret laboratories still keep samples of the virus, under strict security. And the last person ever to die from smallpox was a young woman who caught the virus at a British research lab in 1978.

Beating smallpox was one of the most amazing medical achievements of all time. And today we have vaccines against dozens of other human and animal diseases. There are still some viruses that slip through the net, but every year vaccines save countless lives and prevent untold misery and pain all over the world.

But making safe, effective vaccines is usually a long process. Even after Jenner had developed a safe vaccine for smallpox, it took 200 more years to get rid of the disease altogether.

Luckily, the process is much faster today. We shouldn't

have to wait anything like 200 years for a good vaccine against the COVID-19 virus.

Amazingly, one company downloaded information about the new coronavirus's genes in January 2020 and 25 days later they'd developed a vaccine ready for testing! Normally that would have taken months of work. In the weeks that followed, dozens of other labs came up with their own ingenious plans for COVID-19 vaccines.

But if a vaccine is going to be given to millions, or even billions, of people, there has to be a way to produce a truly massive number of doses so everyone can have a shot. It also has to be tested really carefully until we know it's safe to use.

Things were different in 1885, when the French scientist Louis Pasteur mashed up the dried spinal cord of a rabbit that had been infected with rabies (see p. 81-2), and injected it into the stomach of a nine-year-old boy. It was a desperate measure for a desperate moment: the poor lad had been bitten badly by a rabid dog, and was likely to die very quickly. Pasteur didn't have time to check his new procedure for safety, and, thankfully, the boy made a full recovery.

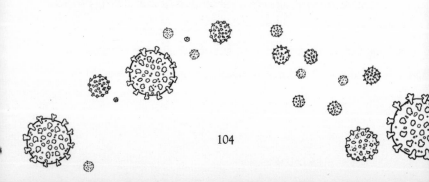

Nobody wants to take that kind of risk these days. Vaccines are amazing, but even when we have them at our disposal, we have to stay on our toes, because these disease-causing viruses have a few more devious tricks up their microscopic sleeves, as we'll see in the next chapter.

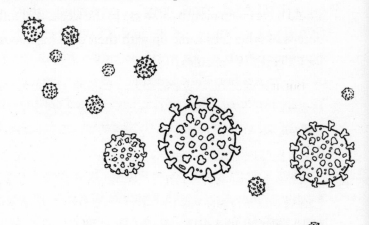

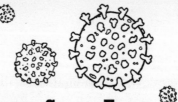

Chapter Seven

Where Viruses Come From

And why they will always come back for more

NEWS FLASH: the 'new' coronavirus that causes COVID-19 isn't 'new' at all. In 2013, way before it started causing mayhem in our world, scientists collected a sample of poo from a horseshoe bat that lived in a cave in China's Yunnan province. The bat poo later turned out to contain a very similar virus* to the one that's causing so many problems today.

They suspect these coronaviruses had been living quite happily in horseshoe bats for hundreds, maybe thousands, of years, without upsetting the bats too much at all. Virologists (that's what we call biologists who study viruses) think the bats' immune systems might have found a way they could exist together, without the virus or the bat going extinct.

I won't bother you if you don't bother me.

Fair enough.

*96% of the information in its RNA genes is identical the COVID-19 virus.

106

No one knows exactly how the COVID-19 virus found its way from bats to humans, but many researchers think it probably happened in a couple of stages. First the virus jumped from the bats to a different kind of wild animal – it could have been a pangolin, a raccoon dog, a civet, or some other creature entirely. It might have stopped off in another species along the way – this virus likes to spread itself around – and from there into people.

Civet
Raccoon dog
Pangolin

Scientists know the bat version of the virus can't easily infect human cells, because its spike 'key' doesn't fit very neatly into our cells' ACE2 'lock' (see p. 23). So something must have happened to change it during its long journey from the bats' caves to human cities. Before it could make its rude entry into human bodies, the virus had to *evolve*.

How the virus changed its spikes

Evolution by natural selection is possibly the most important idea in biology. It explains why some species survive, why others go extinct and how all living things can change – often dramatically – over time.

To see how it works, let's leave viruses for a moment and imagine you live near a forest. One day you release 100 brown stripy beetles and 100 yellow spotty beetles into the forest.

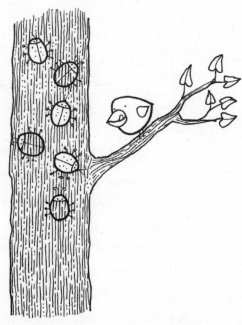

It's more likely the stripy beetles will be hidden from hungry birds and survive – right? They're camouflaged.

So if you went back to the forest a few years later, once the original beetles had bred and made lots of new beetles, you'd probably find mostly stripy beetles.

Now imagine you'd only released yellow spotty beetles into the forest, but very occasionally – and totally randomly – some of those spotty beetles laid a few eggs that grew up into brown stripy beetles. What would happen then?

Birds still gobble up spotty beetles

Oh, hello!

Stripy beetles have an advantage

These stripy beetles have been *naturally selected*.

The rare stripy beetles would be more likely to survive, so there'd be more stripy babies.

So even more years later, when you went back to check, chances are you'd still see mainly stripy beetles on the tree trunks.

Given enough time, spotty beetles might disappear altogether and the population of yellow spotty beetles would have *evolved* into a population of drab-looking stripy beetles.

OK, enough about beetles. I thought we were here to talk about us viruses?

Indeed we are. Be patient.

Evolution by natural selection works on all living things – including viruses. It explains how species adapt themselves so they can continue to survive and thrive, even when their environment changes or they run into new challenges. It explains how giraffes got such long necks for munching high leaves, how kangaroos got so good at jumping, and how we got our opposable thumbs that are great for holding books like this one.

If we swap the beetles for the bat coronaviruses, and the forest for the inside of the human body, then we'll see the same process unfold. If some of those viruses found their way in, and just a tiny minority of them happened to have a spike that fitted snuggly into human ACE2, they would have a massive advantage in the race for survival. The other viruses would just bounce harmlessly off our cells, but a whole new world of opportunity would open up for those few viruses that stuck tight and forced their way in.

But how could a coronavirus's spike suddenly change like that? And how could some viruses have a spike that

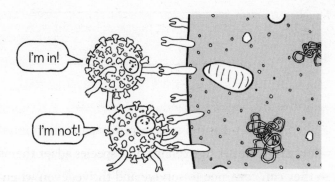

fits ACE2 while others don't?

The answer lies in the genes – those crucial instructions that viruses use to make new viruses and that all living things need to grow and function properly.

Every time a cell copies a set of genes, there's a chance it will make a few mistakes. Think about trying to type an exact copy of all the words in this book. Even the most accurate typist will hit the wrong key from time to time.

Sometimes those little mistakes don't change the meaning of a sentence much, other times a tiny mistake could change it completely.

A single missing 'h' turns 'I hate coronaviruses' into 'I ate coronaviruses', which might have us all a bit worried.

When genes are being copied, the mistakes cells make are called mutations. They usually occur pretty much at random, but they can also be triggered by some chemical poisons or by damaging radiation, like the UV rays in sunlight (yup – that's why it makes sense to apply that sun cream). And the effects mutations have on the cell, creature or virus that inherits them can be good, bad or make no difference at all.

Take the coronavirus gene that has the instructions for building a spike protein. Suppose a new mutation meant only half a spike was built. That would be a bad mutation, because none of the viruses that inherited it would be able to infect any cells. It would be weeded out by natural selection.

A 'good' mutation might be one that helped a virus latch on to its host's cells, even just a tiny bit more effectively than the other viruses without that mutation. Alternatively a new mutation might give a virus the ability to infect the cells of a completely different host species. That could turn out to be a very 'good' mutation too – at least from a virus's point of view – because if that virus did find its way into that new host species, it could discover a whole new universe of cells to spread through.

Virologists think this might well have been what happened to the bat version of the COVID-19 virus. Before it had even infected a single human being, the *bat* virus may have picked up a number of different mutations that just happened to allow it to stick on to and get into *human* cells. Then, when the virus did get inside a human body, natural selection would have made sure any viruses carrying those mutations did very well indeed. Once inside, the virus probably gained further mutations and continued to evolve *after* it first started infecting people. Those changes would have made it even better at invading our cells, avoiding our immune systems, and spreading from one person to the next.

The spillover

When viruses hop from one species into another, scientists call it a spillover event. Nobody knows exactly how often it happens, but most spillovers probably fizzle out quite quickly. For example, the first people who catch the virus might fall ill, but then the virus will probably die out because it hasn't evolved an effective way to jump from person to person.

But sometimes the spillover of a new virus can be the spark that ignites the blazing bonfire of a new epidemic, as happened with the COVID-19 virus at the end of 2019.

We will probably never know exactly how and where the COVID-19 virus originally spilled into our lives, but there are lots of theories.

The wet markets of Wuhan, China, sell all sorts of wild animals for their meat, for fur, for use in traditional medicines and sometimes to keep as pets. Some scientists believe the jump might have happened at one of these markets. Perhaps a butcher was careless about washing his hands . . .

Or it could have happened on a farm. A farmed animal, a pig, perhaps, could have caught the virus from a wild animal. Then the pig could have coughed over a farmworker . . .

For now, we can only make informed guesses. But we know that once it had wheedled its way into the human realm, the virus seized its opportunity. The race was on. It was us, our immune systems and our science, against the COVID-19 virus.

High-speed evolution

For most species, evolution by natural selection seems to take for ever. It certainly took millions of years for giraffes to evolve their long necks, for kangaroos to develop their bounce and for us to evolve our fancy thumbs . . . not to mention our fearsome immune systems. For many viruses, speeding up evolution is their superpower.

Our genes evolve differently from a virus's in three main ways:

---

1. Raw speed

As we know from Chapter 3, viruses rattle through generations much, much faster than humans. So, little changes introduced by gene mutations can quickly start to add up and lead to much bigger changes in how viruses work and how they try to evade our bodies' defences.

2. Attention to detail

When human cells copy their genes, they keep a sharp eye out for any new mutations. If they were copying a book they'd employ the very best professional typists and equip them with spellcheckers and dictionaries too.

For viruses, copying genes can be more like playing a game of 'whispers'. Players sit in a row and the first one whispers a sentence to their neighbour.

Each player repeats the sentence to the player on their left.

Players don't repeat the sentence if anyone doesn't hear it properly, so the last player tells everyone else what they think they heard. The sentence has evolved.

Often it's turned into meaningless gobbledegook, but very occasionally it's like a new line of beautiful poetry. It's usually very funny.

But there's nothing funny about virus evolution. Even if most mutations are 'bad' for viruses, because they reduce parts of the gene instructions to nonsense, that's not necessarily such a problem in a population of trillions. Suppose just a few viruses end up with those 'good' mutations that make them even just a tiny bit more effective, natural selection will make sure those viruses quickly reproduce and thrive.

3. Shuffling genes

Just as dogs have many different breeds but all belong to the same species, each species of virus will usually come in various 'strains' that are closely related but distinct. It's their gene mutations that make them work in slightly different ways. And viral strains can be blended in the same way dogs can be crossbred – e.g. when a cocker spaniel is crossed with a miniature poodle to make a cockapoo.

Sometimes two different strains of the virus infect the same cell.

The genes of each strain get mixed up.

New viruses inherit a random mix of the characteristics of their 'parent' viruses.

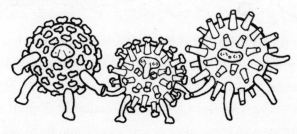

Not all viruses can reshuffle their genes like this, but the coronaviruses and the ones that cause flu seem to be rather good at it. And sometimes this viral gene shuffling creates a completely new strain of virus with new ways of infecting their hosts and hijacking cells.

Viral problem solvers

Because they can accelerate evolution, viruses are like moving targets, always changing their ways and coming up with new tricks. That's probably why a famous virologist called

Professor George Klein once told a room full of extremely brilliant virologists that: 'Even the stupidest virus is cleverer than the cleverest virologist.'

See! What did I tell you? I'm a genius! Even Professor Klein thinks so.

Yes, but thinking is something you definitely can't do. That's not what he meant by 'clever'.

It's the fact that viruses solve problems and cook up new tactics by evolving so quickly that makes them seem cleverer than us. The COVID-19 virus has certainly devised some cunning ways to try to alter or avoid our immune responses.

For example, it's thought the virus has a way to block the production of interferon – the cytokine many cells make when they realize they are infected by viruses (see p. 54). That's a particularly devious thing to do, since interferon is one of the signals that fires up our immune systems in the first place.

Speedy evolution is also part of the reason immunity doesn't last very long for some viruses. By the time memory B-cells and T-cells meet a fast-evolving virus again, perhaps a year or more after infection or vaccination, the virus could have changed so much that they don't even recognize it as a threat. That's one of the reasons why scientists develop a new flu vaccination every winter.

Memory B- and T-cells

As well as mutating quickly, flu viruses can zip back and forth between people and other animals quite regularly. And when they come back after a new round of gene shuffling, they can behave like a completely new strain.

All this speeded-up evolution probably sounds a bit alarming, and it certainly makes it more of a challenge to design good antiviral medicines and vaccines. But viruses don't always evolve to become nastier.

If a virus cares about anything at all, it's survival and reproduction. Damaging its host's body is not the virus's main ambition, and killing that body may not be in its interests at all, since that will often reduce the chances of a virus spreading to other people. That's why some of the most 'successful' viruses – which reproduce fastest and spread furthest – are the ones that cause the mildest symptoms. Common cold viruses often do really well because most people they infect don't get poorly enough to stay at home. Instead, they muddle on with their normal lives infecting lots of other people along the way.

Up to a quarter of colds are caused by coronaviruses, and some virologists think some of those viruses might've started out as deadlier strains, which then evolved to become less dangerous. It's possible that the COVID-19 virus could evolve to become milder, but we definitely shouldn't count on that happening.

In fact, for the time being, the COVID-19 virus doesn't seem to be evolving very rapidly. That's probably because these coronaviruses take a bit more care over gene copying than many other kinds of virus do. One of the proteins they make has evolved the ability to spot and correct some of the new mutations as they appear. That's good news for us. It means scientists have a chance to work out what we're up against before the virus has another bright idea and changes its spikes, or its tactics, again.

We can't stop viruses evolving, but there's quite a lot we can do to make spillovers less likely, or less damaging.

And that's important because the sudden appearance of the COVID-19 virus has reminded us that there's always another virus looking for its chance to leap out of the woods like a microscopic bandit and try its luck against us.

Don't provoke the viruses

Scientists estimate that there could be as many as 800,000 virus species lurking in the world's forests, swamps, caves and savannahs, which all have the potential to spillover and infect humans. Working out how to keep these viruses in the wild should be a big priority for everyone, because however bad the COVID-19 virus is, the next new virus could be worse.

Spillovers are still rare – thank goodness – but some virologists worry that they're happening more often today than they did in the past. And whose fault is that? Well, scientists don't blame the bats. They blame humans.

There's no one person or country that's responsible. Thanks to the evolution of our big brains, handy thumbs and nifty immune systems, humans happen to be an incredibly successful species. There are more people alive now than ever before, and in many parts of the world we're steadily getting richer. In many ways this is great: fewer people go hungry,

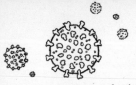

more people have work, more children go to school, and every year more of us have access to healthcare.

But it also means people need more of everything: more food, more money, more T-shirts, more cars, more houses, more smartphones, and so on. We cut down forests for timber, clear land for farming, dig into the ground for oil and minerals. We build new roads through pristine jungles. We drain swamps and fell woods to build new suburbs. Farms get bigger and bigger.

None of this is only 'good' or only 'bad'. The point is, because we dominate the whole of Earth, millions of people are regularly coming into contact with millions of other non-human animals, and each of these animals can carry lots of different viruses. And, as we know, all it takes for a spillover to happen is a squirt of blood, an untimely sneeze or the bite of an insect.

It sounds terrifying, but keep breathing and read on, because there is actually quite a lot we can do to make spillovers less common, and to massively reduce the chances of them triggering deadly pandemics when they do happen. We can:

1. Cut back on the plundering of Earth's resources. More recycling, more reusing, more mending, more renewable energy, and even more vegetarianism, could all help: it would all mean less need for people to rub up against wild viruses.

2. Protect Earth's remaining wildernesses. A lot less hunting, trapping, logging and road-building wouldn't just reduce the spillover risk, it would help tackle extinctions of all kinds of other species and benefit the climate as well.

3. Hunt out the viruses. Researchers found the new coronavirus in 2013 because they were actually looking for new viruses. With samples of animal poo or blood, virus hunters can scan for virus genes in their labs. Then they can read the information in those genes to identify all the different viruses present. If we don't know which viruses are out there, we have no way of knowing which ones could leap into our world next.

4. Find out how wild viruses work. That way virologists can predict which ones we need to worry about: the ones that are most likely to be able to infect us and cause epidemics.

5. Design our own defences *before* spillovers happen. Researchers could actually get busy inventing tests to identify new viral infections, and even planning vaccines and medicines against them so when the next new virus pops up, we're ready for it.

6. Spot and stop the spillovers. Hunters, loggers, miners, farmers, wet market traders and everyone else who spends time in wild places or with animals could all help by being extra careful with their hygiene and reporting any strange illnesses.

Some of these things are already happening and it's all totally achievable stuff. But we need to be doing much more of it. There's no other way to nip spillovers in the bud before they start causing havoc.

There are an awful lot of viruses out there, but they certainly aren't all bad guys, as we'll see in the next chapter.

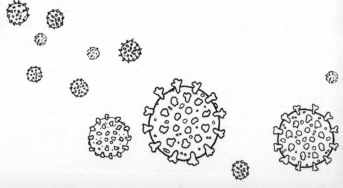

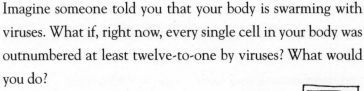

Chapter Eight

A World of Viruses

Meet some of the good guys

Imagine someone told you that your body is swarming with viruses. What if, right now, every single cell in your body was outnumbered at least twelve-to-one by viruses? What would you do?

- Run straight to the doctor?
- Jump into a giant bath full of industrial-strength disinfectant?

Well, don't be too hasty, because all of the above is true. And it's perfectly normal.

Even when we're in tip-top good health, there are hundreds of trillions of viruses in your body, on your body and all around you at all times. Most of these viruses can be deadly killers, but – luckily – hardly any of them can actually infect your cells, or do you any harm.

Believe it or not, a lot of the viruses inside your body are good for you. Your body actually welcomes many of them aboard.

Take the snot in your nose, for example, viruses love the stuff. It isn't just that snot traps unwanted germs to stop them getting into your system (see p. 41). There's another whole set of viruses that hang out in your nose too. They latch on tight to your snot, because it protects them. And, in return, these viruses help to protect you.

How do they do that? By attacking bacteria. There are all sorts of bacteria that can give humans really nasty infections and diseases, and your body seems to enlist these viruses to fend them off.

Yes, this really does mean that *bacteria get ill too*. In fact, viruses that infect bacteria are far more common than all those that cause disease in animals and plants put together. Biologists call them bacteriophages, or just 'phages' for short, and there are millions of different species of them.

Phages take their murderous work very seriously. When they infect bacteria, they often produce so many new phages that the bacterial cell is simply torn apart. Which is great news for you, because that helps prevent or get rid of bacterial infections.

Your body is actually so fond of phages that it doesn't just encourage them to hang out in your nose; you've got them all over the place. Virologists suspect there are vast numbers of them lurking in the thin layers of mucus that coat all of your body's inside surfaces: including your mouth, trachea, lungs and urinary tract (where your pee comes out). There are even larger swarms of them inside your gut.

This is all-out biological warfare: your body recruits these viruses and uses them as a deadly shield that can kill bacteria that stray too close. So these phages actually form part of your immune system!

Traitor, I thought it was viruses vs humans!

It's a pretty effective strategy too, but your body has to keep close control over its phage army. There's no way you'd want them to zap all the bacteria in your body because, as with viruses, some bacteria are very helpful:

- Bacteria in our intestines help us digest food – without them, most of the fruit and veg we eat would just pass straight on through, taking their nutrients with them.
- Bacteria produce vitamins and other chemicals that your body urgently needs, but can't make for itself.

- And bacteria in our gut help to keep our immune systems, and even our brains, working at their full potential.

So an outright massacre would be a very bad idea. That's why your body seems to produce mucus in a way that is very attractive to the kind of phages that frazzle the dangerous bacteria: it's a way of inviting these viruses inside. Far from being our enemies, bacteria-beating viruses are our friends.

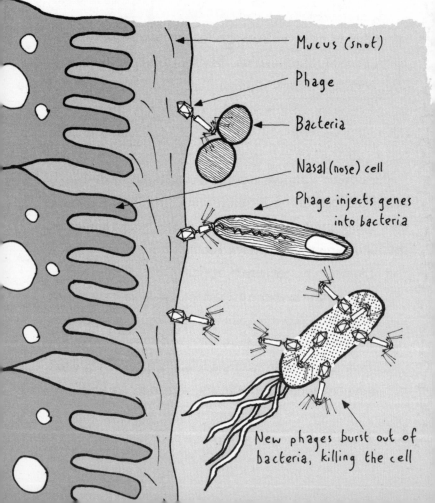

Mucus (snot)

Phage

Bacteria

Nasal (nose) cell

Phage injects genes into bacteria

New phages burst out of bacteria, killing the cell

The virus doctors

Isabelle Carnell-Holdaway was 15 in 2017 when she was finally called in to hospital for a lung transplant. She'd spent most of her life struggling with cystic fibrosis, a painful health condition that can affect various organs of the body, but causes particular damage to the lungs. A lung transplant is a big operation, but if it was successful, life was going to be much, much easier for Isabelle.

The transplant did go well, but unfortunately some of Isabelle's scars just didn't heal. It seemed they were infected with bacteria. Usually antibiotic medicines clear bacterial infections very effectively, and the doctors tried various different ones, but none of them helped Isabelle's wounds heal. Soon the infection was spreading all over her body.

With her life in danger, Isabelle's mum came up with a daring plan: could her doctors try using a virus to tackle the bacteria? By testing lots of different phages, they found three species of virus that killed the bacteria in Isabelle's wounds, and began to inject them into her bloodstream twice a day.

Just three days later the painful sores were starting to heal and within six weeks the infection had almost disappeared. In the end Isabelle's condition improved and in 2020 she said, 'I can go out with my friends, study, have fun… I feel the most normal I have ever felt.'

Isabelle's infection was resistant to antibiotics, the medicines that usually treat infections caused by bacteria. Antibiotics first became available less than a century ago, but in that time they've probably saved more lives than any other kind of medicine. However, antibiotic-resistant infections are affecting more people every year, with some of them becoming impossible to treat. This is a huge problem for all of us. Without effective antibiotics, it's possible that even a minor wound, like a small scratch from a rose thorn, could get infected by resistant bacteria and turn into a fatal disease.

Researchers are desperately looking for new ways to deal with these dangerous microbes, so the fact that Isabelle's virus-based therapy seemed to go well was great news. Scientists still have a lot of work to do to prove that phages are effective and safe, but because they can identify and destroy their bacterial targets with laser-like accuracy, some scientists hope that one day phages might help solve the problem of antibiotic resistance.

Life-sustaining viruses

Viruses have been on this planet far, far longer than humans have. They've quite possibly existed for as long as life itself, and can infect the cells of pretty much any species you can think of, from aardvarks to alligators, from mushrooms to magpies, and from tulips to tarantulas. Wherever life exists, viruses will thrive.

Until really quite recently, most biologists didn't think many viruses existed in seawater. But when they actually started looking, they got a big surprise. If you scoop up a teaspoonful of water from near the surface of any ocean, it will probably contain up to 100 million viruses. So every time you swim in the sea, you'll probably swallow as many viruses as there are people living in the USA!

And if you add up all those virus-laden spoonfuls of water, you quickly realize that the world's seas contain an astronomical number of viruses. Actually, 'astronomical' isn't the best word to choose, because there are a hundred times more viruses in the oceans than there are stars in the entire universe.

The latest estimates say there are about:

4,000,000,000,000,000, 000,000,000,000,000

(that's 4 followed by 30 zeroes, which is such a stupendously big number that mathematicians give it a stupendously silly name: four nonillion).

What do all these viruses do all day? Mainly, they kill lots and lots of the bacteria and other single-celled microbes that live in the seas. These non-viral microbes do all sorts of things to help keep the oceans functioning properly: they capture the sun's energy, break down waste and are the favourite foodstuff for all kinds of larger marine life forms. These microbes are also extremely abundant. If you were to weigh everything that's living in the oceans, the combined weight of all single-celled microbes would be three times heavier than that of all the larger, more visible living things – all the fish, whales, dolphins, jellyfish, seaweed and everything else in the ocean – put together.

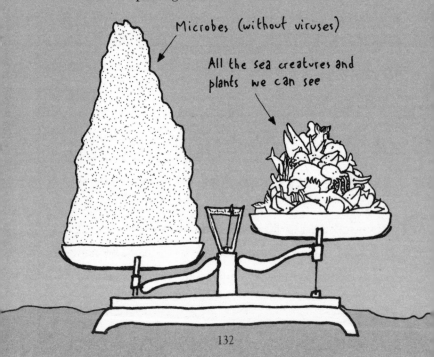

Microbes (without viruses)

All the sea creatures and plants we can see

That's an awful lot of microbes. Viruses don't weigh as much, but there are even more of them. And because of all those viruses it's thought that a trillion trillion bacteria die in the ocean every second. Altogether viruses slaughter 20–40% of all the ocean's larger non-viral microbes every day.

If you happened to be one of those microbes, that wouldn't seem like a good thing at all. But biologists think all that killing is a very good thing indeed for most other life in the seas – and, in fact, for the whole planet.

Here's why:

1. Viruses massively increase the variety of life forms that thrive in the ocean. Without viruses, microbes would just keep growing until they'd hoovered up all the nutrients in the seas. Then the microbes would starve, and so would everything else. So what actually happens when a particular microbe population flourishes is that viruses infect and kill its cells. That pushes the microbe population back down to a more manageable level and gives all the other kinds of ocean life a chance to grow instead. As well as this, the constant virus attacks create a kind of soup-like slurry of dead and damaged microbes, which acts like a fertilizer to turbocharge the growth of all kinds of other ocean microbes. Those little creatures then provide endless tasty meals for fish, corals, whales and many other organisms. The end result is more vibrant and diverse marine life. (see pp. 136–137)

2. Viruses help make the oxygen we breathe. Almost all life on Earth depends on a chemical reaction you might have heard of: photosynthesis. This is when specialized structures and chemicals in plants, algae and bacteria use energy from sunlight to transform water and carbon dioxide gas into energy-rich sugars and carbohydrates, in other words, food. This reaction has a vitally important by-product: oxygen. We'd be stuffed without it.

Did you know that more than half of the planet's photosynthesis actually happens in the oceans? A lot of it is done by a kind of bacteria called cyanobacteria. Some of the most common cyanobacteria can only photosynthesize when they've been infected by a particular virus. Without crucial virus genes, these cyanobacteria can't capture sunlight. The virus benefits from this, because this ensures its host has enough energy to make new viruses, but we all benefit from the

extra oxygen the cyanobacteria end up producing too. In fact, you can thank these viruses for at least one out of every ten lungfuls of air you breathe! (see pp. 136–137)

3. Viruses slow down global warming. Lots of the larger marine microbes, such as algae and other plankton*, protect themselves by building tough shell-like coats that surround their cells. They need carbon to make these shells, and all of that carbon originally comes from carbon dioxide gas, which is absorbed out of the atmosphere during photosynthesis. When viruses kill these microbes, their tiny shells can sink straight to the bottom of the oceans, taking the carbon they're made from with them. Although the sunken microbes are each truly minuscule, they die in such vast numbers that it's equivalent to burying billions of tonnes of carbon dioxide on the seabed. Scientists think this process actually soaks up a significant chunk of the carbon dioxide we humans produce each year by burning fossil fuels in cars, trucks, ships, planes, factories and power stations. (see pp. 136–137)

*Plankton is a general term used to describe the microscopic life that floats in seawater, including tiny plants and algae that photosynthesize and small animals, as well as all the bacteria and viruses.

Shells of dead microbes

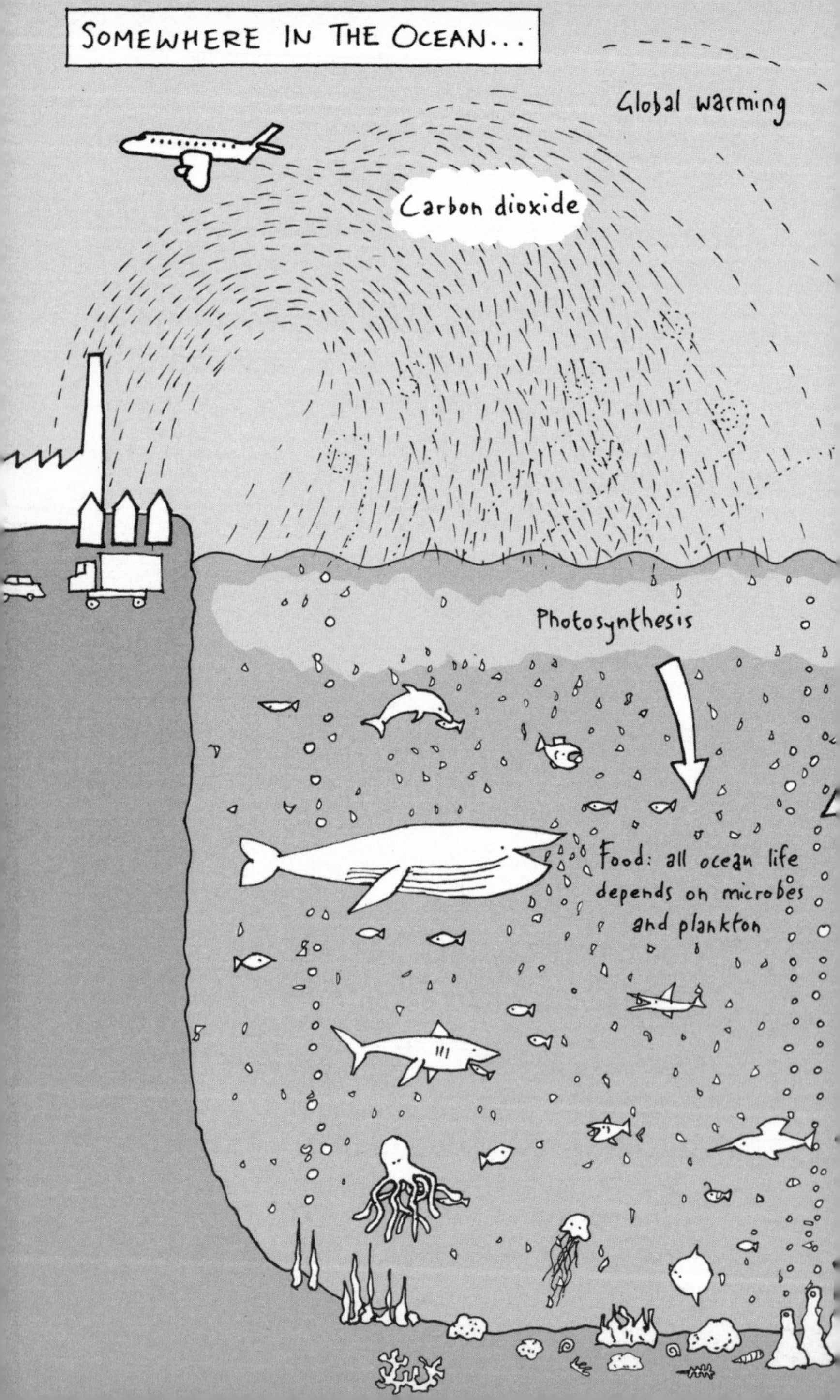
SOMEWHERE IN THE OCEAN...
Global warming
Carbon dioxide
Photosynthesis
Food: all ocean life depends on microbes and plankton

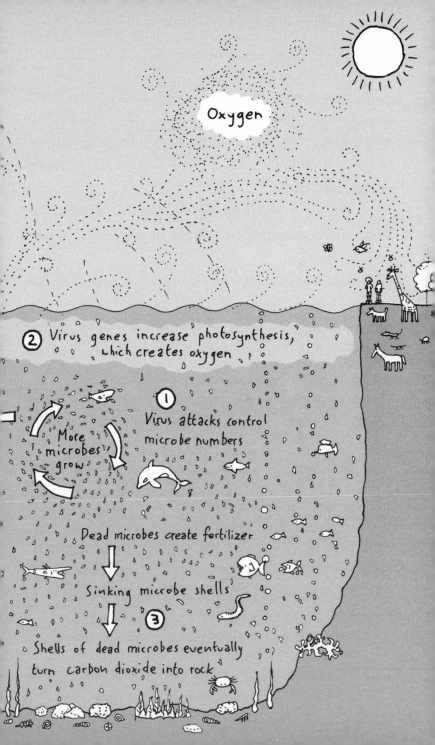

Oxygen

(2) Virus genes increase photosynthesis, which creates oxygen

(1) Virus attacks control microbe numbers

More microbes grow

Dead microbes create fertilizer

Sinking microbe shells

(3)

Shells of dead microbes eventually turn carbon dioxide into rock

Without viruses, the climate crisis would probably get much worse, much more quickly. Some researchers even wonder whether it might be possible to give these viruses a boost so they actually help stop the planet getting dangerously hot.

In short, if it wasn't for all the viruses in the seas, the Earth would soon start overheating, running out of oxygen and, er, dying.

Viruses have a huge, and often positive, impact on life on dry land too. Stupendously big numbers of them exist in soil, for example. So far, we know even less about these than we know about the newly discovered ocean viruses, but they almost certainly help make and maintain the soil itself. That means we might have to thank viruses for almost all of the oxygen we breathe, since almost all plants on Earth need *earth* to grow in.

And where viruses are concerned, maybe that's the biggest riddle of all: without the death and destruction they cause, life as a whole couldn't flourish in such incredible diversity.

So, all you viral eco-warriors, please take a bow.

Really, it's nothing.

Not you, coronavirus, there's no silver lining to your cloud.

The viruses that make you, you (and ewes, ewes)

If *thinking* killer viruses for the continued existence of the life that grows in the soil and the seas sounds strange to you, things are about to get even stranger.

Brace yourselves, these next two facts might come as a bit of a shock.

First, your body is not just full of viruses, *you are part virus*. About 9% of the DNA in each of your cells is actually virus DNA. (Not just you *personally*; it's the same for everyone!)

Second, if a virus hadn't infected one of your ancestors millions of years ago, you could never have been born.

These facts are linked, but let's start by looking at them one at a time.

Almost all the virus DNA found in your cells was put there a long, long time ago by a group of viruses called retroviruses. When a retrovirus infects a cell, it makes a copy of its genes and inserts them into the host cell's DNA, mixing them among the host's genes. Once this happens, the viral genes usually stay there for ever, which means they often get passed on from one generation of organisms to the next. Retroviruses have been infecting cells for nearly 500 million years (way before the dinosaurs went extinct 65 million years ago). It took millions of years for humans to evolve and during that time retroviruses infected our distant pre-human ancestors so many times that scientists today can identify around 100,000 different chunks of our DNA that originally came from retroviruses. So nearly a tenth of your DNA is actually the leftover relics of past virus infections!

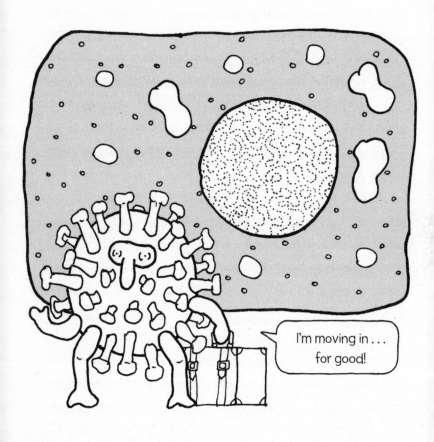

This brings us to the second point. Although almost all of the retrovirus genes in our DNA have lost the ability to reawaken and make new viruses, some of them can still make proteins (the worker molecules all life forms need, see p. 30). Occasionally the host cell finds those virus proteins rather useful. There's one in particular that is totally crucial for building the placenta that linked you and your mum when you were in her womb.

In fact, if it wasn't for that vital retrovirus gene, the placenta might never have evolved at all. And if that hadn't happened, we'd have almost no mammals* in our world at all. That means no anteaters, no baboons, no cats, no dogs, no elephants, no three-toed sloths, no blue whales, no ewes, and no *you*.

I don't know what to say. I feel a bit humbled to hear that we viruses have done so much for you.

Don't even try to claim credit for any of this, coronavirus. None of it happened thanks to *you*.

* Duck-billed platypuses and echidnas would be OK since they lay eggs, so their embryos don't need a placenta.

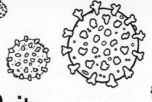

Chapter Nine
Let's Call it Quits
Learning to live with viruses, good and bad

There are no two ways about it, viruses are weird. Most biologists can't even decide whether they're alive or dead.

Some argue that viruses are just too small and too simple to be considered proper living things. They point out that, when they're outside cells, viruses can't do anything at all. They seem no more alive than a crystal of salt. And, as we know, their bodies are less complex than those of even the simplest living cells. As the famous biologist Sir Peter Medawar once put it, a virus is no more than 'a piece of bad news wrapped up in protein'.

'Wrapped in protein'? You might've won a Nobel Prize, Sir Peter, but you're forgetting all that lipid in my envelope. We viruses are not as simple as you might think.

Good point, coronavirus. And whenever scientists think they're getting a grip on you viruses, you have a nasty habit of throwing up a new surprise. Either a virus mutates and changes its ways, or a new one shows up, as if from nowhere, and starts breaking all the rules.

Meet the giant viruses

In 2019 researchers stumbled across a whole set of new and radically different kinds of phage (those viruses that infect bacteria). They found them lurking all over the place: in rivers, in dirt, in hot springs, at the bottom of mine shafts, even in people's mouths and in their poo.

The first shocking thing about these new viruses is their size: they're ten times bigger than the other phages that live inside our bodies. (OK, so *giant* is an exaggeration – the largest of these monsters is still ten times smaller than one of your red blood cells.)

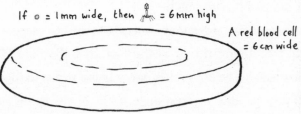

If ⚬ = 1mm wide, then 🦠 = 6mm high

A red blood cell = 6 cm wide

A hair from your hand under a microscope = 15 cm wide ⟶

These whopping great phages also have a huge number of genes – not as many as the 20,000 genes in our cells, but 20–30 times more than the COVID-19 virus has. And they use those genes to do some extraordinary and unexpected things.

Working a bit like tiny engineers, they rejig the machinery of the cells they've infected, snipping out bits of the host's DNA and reprogramming the cell to do exactly what the phage wants it to do. These giant phages take the art of hijack to a whole new level.

And – most surprising of all – these viruses come equipped with their own version of an immune system! If any other virus dares to barge in and try to share the same host cell, these giant phages spot them coming and deploy molecules that act as minuscule weaponized 'scissors'. Soon the rival virus will find that its precious genes have been cut into useless little pieces.

Just a few years ago nobody would have even guessed a virus could do such a sophisticated thing. So can we really say viruses are simple? Not so much.

The other main argument scientists use to suggest viruses can't be living things is the fact that they are all total freeloaders. To be alive, they say, a being needs to look after itself and be able to reproduce itself. It has to be an *independent* life form.

Well, it's time to introduce you to an even bigger giant virus, the Megavirus, which is also relatively new to science. These guys infect amoebas*, rather than bacteria. They still need that cell's help to reproduce themselves, but these viruses appear to do a lot more of the actual virus-copying and virus-

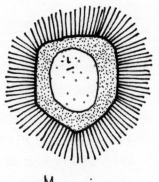

Megavirus

constructing work for themselves. When they infect an amoeba, they build a complicated structure called a virus factory inside it. Raw materials go in at one end, and new genes and virus proteins emerge at the other. In some ways, it's a bit like a cell within a cell.

And like the phages we've just met, these giant viruses have evolved a similar kind of immune system. The amazing thing is, they are defending *themselves* from other smaller viruses that want to hijack the giant's virus factory. Crazy as it might seem, even viruses can be infected by viruses . . .

So it's quite possible that, right now, in somebody's guts there are viruses that are infecting viruses that are infecting amoebas that are infecting humans . . .

*Amoebas are single-celled organisms that move about and catch food by
making finger-like bulges in their outer membranes. Some are parasites that
can exist in animals' intestines.

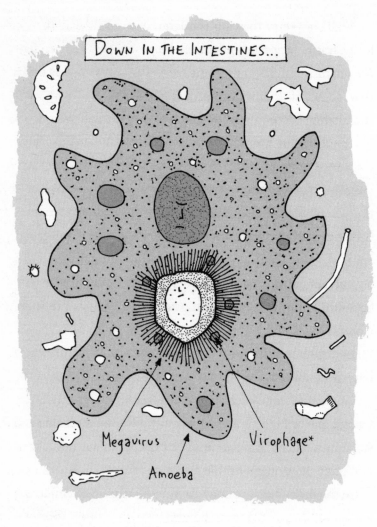

*Virophages are small viruses that can only reproduce when their host cell is infected by a larger virus.

That's a pretty dizzying thought. It would mean there'd be a parasite that's dependent on a parasite, that's dependent on a parasite, that's dependent on a person. Does that mean that some of these microscopic creatures are *more alive* than others? Does it make sense to call any of them truly independent life forms?

Hey, it's not like you guys are totally independent life forms either! You wouldn't last long without all those plants and animals you're always chewing on, would you?

You've got me stumped there, virus. We humans do depend on all sorts of other living things. Pretty sure we're alive, though . . .

But as for viruses, who knows? Maybe that's another one of your fiendish riddles.

Could viruses be both alive and dead: lifeless when they're outside the cell but very much alive when they get inside and start reproducing? Or perhaps they occupy some mysterious twilight zone in-between life and non-life?

In the end, where we draw the dividing line between living and non-living things may be a matter of opinion. But one thing we can all agree on is that viruses are a fact of life, and indeed a part of life. Viruses are everywhere at all times; some are our friends, some are our foes. And if we can't avoid them altogether – and we certainly can't destroy them altogether – perhaps we need to find a way to live alongside them without constantly giving them new chances to do us harm.

Viruses are like the weather

Since the COVID-19 virus barged into our world and went on the rampage, it's made a lot of people very miserable, very confused and sometimes very angry. People talk about fighting back against viruses and even waging war on them, and it's easy to understand why, given how much pain and disruption they cause.

But declaring war on viruses would be a bit like declaring war on the weather. We can and must protect ourselves and fight off individual outbreaks and pandemics, just as we must do all we can to defend ourselves against typhoons, floods and blizzards. But when it comes to the crunch, nobody has the power to stop a storm in its tracks.

On the other hand, humans have never been in a better position to cope with the assaults viruses make on our bodies:

- Viruses were invisible, but now we can see them – and their inner workings too – with the help of testing kits, electron microscopes and all sorts of

148

other high-tech scientific devices.

- We knew very little about them, but now we can study them in labs and hospitals, learn how they work, understand how they spread, and change our behaviour to slow them down or stop them.

- For thousands of years we had no cures, but we're getting better all the time at designing medicines and vaccines that can ward viruses off.

With every new pandemic we get a bit better at dealing with viruses too. But, the truth is, just as there will always be another storm, there will always be another disease-causing virus. And just as rain will always 'try' to make us wet, viruses will always 'try' to get into our cells. We can't blame the rain, and we can't really *blame* the viruses. It's just the way they are.

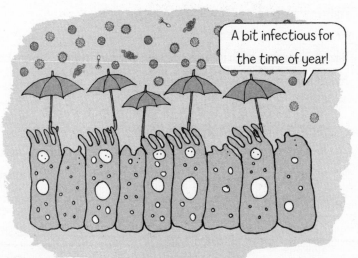

And if we look at the world from a virus's point of view, it's obvious that humans are brilliant hosts to choose, even with our powerful virus-killing immune systems. There are already nearly eight billion of us on Earth, with more babies being born all the time. Most of us live pretty close together in cities – within easy hopping distance. And, thanks to our daily journeys to school or work, and the planes and boats that ceaselessly move us, food and everything else to all the corners of the globe, there's plenty of scope for any ambitious virus to have a pretty good shot at infecting everyone.

What's more, we're generally getting better and better at keeping ourselves healthy, well fed and alive. That's good for humans, but it's also good for viruses: it means there are even more cells they can try to infect.

Fighting viruses *and* the climate crisis

We can't stop whirlwinds, floods or heatwaves, but that doesn't mean we can't influence what the weather will do in the future.

After all, we've already altered the atmosphere so much that the planet is getting warmer. The climate crisis we've created is changing weather patterns and harming people and wildlife across the globe. It might even be

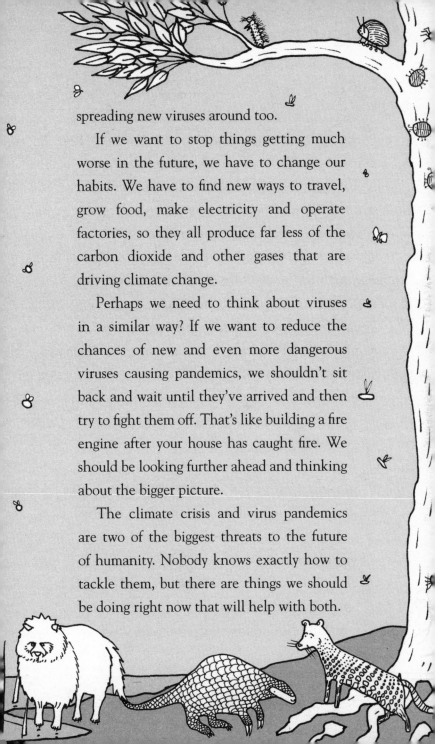

spreading new viruses around too.

If we want to stop things getting much worse in the future, we have to change our habits. We have to find new ways to travel, grow food, make electricity and operate factories, so they all produce far less of the carbon dioxide and other gases that are driving climate change.

Perhaps we need to think about viruses in a similar way? If we want to reduce the chances of new and even more dangerous viruses causing pandemics, we shouldn't sit back and wait until they've arrived and then try to fight them off. That's like building a fire engine after your house has caught fire. We should be looking further ahead and thinking about the bigger picture.

The climate crisis and virus pandemics are two of the biggest threats to the future of humanity. Nobody knows exactly how to tackle them, but there are things we should be doing right now that will help with both.

Learning to enjoy nature for what it is, and doing much more to protect it would be a great start. That way the planet's forests and oceans could get on with all that carbon-absorbing, oxygen-producing magic that sustains all life. And if we can stop exploiting the last remaining wildernesses and jungles, we'll end up with fewer viruses hopping into our world.

Eating a bit less meat and dairy could help too: giving less land over to cattle would stop huge farms from spreading into wildlife habitats, potentially causing spillovers. Most intensive livestock farms also produce a lot of the greenhouse gases that are damaging the environment. So do planes, trucks, ships and most cars. Cutting back on carbon-fuelled travel that isn't strictly necessary wouldn't just reduce harmful emissions, it would slow the spread of viruses too.

And, just as we need to understand much more about the complicated ways that the gases in the atmosphere affect the weather and the climate as a whole, we have to throw ourselves into learning everything we can about viruses. Knowing what viruses are out there and how they work is our only hope of turning the roar of the next deadly virus into a feeble whimper.

Our understanding gets a little bit better all the time, but we've still got a lot to learn.

And perhaps there are some things the viruses can actually teach us?

Go on, ask me anything: Coronavirus the Mighty at your service.

Well, I doubt you can help, virus. Nothing can heal the tragedies you've brought into our homes. But, who knows, maybe something positive can eventually grow out of it all?

Could it finally remind us that life is fragile and far more precious than anything else? After all, it only takes a meagre pinprick of RNA, protein and lipid to steal the people we love from us, stop whole countries and turn our everyday existences upside down.

The COVID-19 virus forced us to slow down and stop. We don't have to go straight back to our old ways. Maybe the virus has given us a chance to see a different future – a future where everyone can get the healthcare, support and the opportunities that they need. A future where today's climate crisis doesn't turn into tomorrow's climate catastrophe.

Because, at the end of the day, no other creature cares a fig about what happens to humans. It's up to us to change.

Er, but if you lot got wiped out, I'd need to find a new home. Suppose I could always go back to the bats . . .

You'd cope, virus.

But really, if we want to find a way to keep sharing this planet with viruses, but not have them cause too much trouble, there's one thing we really must do.

We need to keep solving their riddles.

Glossary

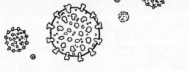

ACE2/ACE2 lock/receptor a protein attached to the outside of many of our body's cells that helps keep our blood pressure healthy. Some coronaviruses use it to recognize and infect our cells.

AIDS (acquired immunodeficiency syndrome) a disease caused by viruses that can weaken the body's ability to protect itself.

algae creatures that aren't plants, but which can photosynthesize. They mostly live in water as single-celled microbes or larger seaweeds.

antibiotic a medicine used to treat infections caused by bacteria.

antibody a molecule made by B-cells that can recognize and stick to substances (called antigens) that threaten the immune system.

antiviral a medicine used to treat viral infections.

bacteria a large and highly varied group of single-celled microbes.

bacteriophage viruses that infect bacteria. Often called 'phages'.

B-cell immune system cell that produces antibodies.

cell the smallest thing that is definitively 'alive'. Cells can live as single-celled organisms, or as parts of an animal, plant or fungus.

climate crisis serious problems due to the warming of our planet's surface, caused by human activities that lead to the build-up of carbon dioxide, methane and other greenhouse gases in the atmosphere.

coronavirus a kind of virus that can cause diseases in humans or other animals, often by infecting cells in the airways.

COVID-19 illness an infectious disease caused by a particular kind of coronavirus, first diagnosed in 2019.

COVID-19 virus the virus that causes the COVID-19 illness. Its scientific name is severe acute respiratory syndrome coronavirus 2, or SARS-CoV-2.

cyanobacteria bacteria that can photosynthesize.

cytokine a chemical substance used for communication between the different cells of the immune system.

DNA (deoxyribonucleic acid) the stuff that genes are made from in all cells and all life forms, apart from certain viruses (those with RNA genes).

electron microscope a super-powerful microscope that uses a beam of electrons rather than light to reveal extremely small objects.

epidemic an outbreak of an infectious disease that affects a large number of people in the same place at the same time.

epidemiologist a scientist who studies epidemics.

evolve/evolution the way living things gradually change their appearance and inner workings over time.

exponential growth when a population grows at a rate that gets faster and faster all the time. If each new generation is always exactly twice the size of the previous one, it is called exponential doubling.

fungus mushrooms, yeast, toadstools, mildews, moulds and infections like 'athlete's foot'. They all feed on decaying material or other living things.

gene part of a living thing that contains a specific instruction for how to build or operate a certain aspect of a cell, virus or body. It usually works by controlling the production of a specific kind of protein molecule.

global warming see climate crisis.

growth rate how quickly a population grows. Used to calculate how much bigger each new generation is compared to the previous one.

HIV-1 the most common of the retroviruses that can cause AIDS.

host a cell or body that a parasite or pathogen lives in or infects.

immunity a body's ability to resist a particular infection.

interferon a kind of cytokine, often produced by virus-infected cells.

membrane a microscopic layer of lipid and protein molecules that surrounds and protects all living cells, and some viruses.

memory cell a B-cell or a T-cell that can survive for months, years or decades and can rapidly kick-start an immune response to a pathogen that a body has encountered before.

microbe a living thing too small to see without a microscope.

mucus thick, slimy liquid produced by a body to protect delicate surfaces, such as the mouth, nose, throat and digestive system.

mutation a change in the structure of a gene that can be passed from a living thing to its offspring.

natural selection a process that drives evolution. Individuals born with characteristics that suit their environment stand a better chance of survival. As they produce more offspring, those characteristics become more common.

nucleocapsid protein a chemical substance found in some kinds of virus that protects their genes, coiling them up to fit inside the virus.

opposable opposable thumbs can press against fingers to grip or pinch.

pandemic an epidemic that has spread across continents, or the world.

parasite a life form that lives on or inside another living thing, getting food or other benefits from its host without giving anything back.

pathogen something that causes infection; often called a germ.

phage see bacteriophage.

phagocyte a cell that can swallow whole objects, including viruses, bacteria or the body's own dead cells.

photosynthesis a chemical process that uses energy from the sun to convert carbon dioxide and water into sugar and oxygen.

placenta a structure inside a mother's womb that ensures oxygen and nutrients can be passed from the mother's blood to her growing baby.

plankton trillions of different small and microscopic organisms that drift around in the oceans.

pneumonia a serious illness that causes the lungs to start filling up with fluid, making it difficult to breathe properly.

protein large molecules that are essential for all living things. They have many functions in cells and viruses, including building structures, controlling chemical reactions and sending and receiving messages.

red blood cell a disc-shaped cell that carries oxygen from the lungs to all other cells in the body.

reproduction producing exact copies of a virus or living cell, or making a new generation of organisms.

ribosome structure found in all living cells that turns the instructions genes carry into molecules of protein.

RNA (ribonucleic acid) a chemical with a similar structure to DNA. Present in all living cells, it forms the genes of certain viruses.

spillover the moment when a virus or other pathogen passes from one host species into the members of a different host species.

stratosphere an extremely windy and cold layer of gases in Earth's atmosphere between 10 and 50 kilometres above the planet's surface.

T-cell a kind of white blood cell that launches very specific attacks on infections and sometimes on cancers.

vaccine something that can be put into our bodies to mimic a real infection to trigger an immune response. Vaccinations give people or animals long-lasting protection against the real pathogen.

verruca an infectious wart that can grow on feet.

virus a small pathogen that can only reproduce itself inside the cells of a different living thing.

white blood cell cells of the immune system, produced in your bone marrow, that move out through your blood to protect almost every part of your body.

Acknowledgements

This book hurtled from idea to reality in less than four months. That would've been impossible if not for an incredible team of collaborators.

Eternal thanks to editor Helen Greathead for her vision, her tireless hard work, and her continuous supply of ideas, reassurance and incisive comments. Immense gratitude to Alison Gadsby. Working at record-breaking speed and always with the greatest humour, she somehow imposed order and style on a constantly evolving mass of words and pictures. Big thanks to Anthony Hinton for astute editorial input and deft project management throughout. Also to Julia Bruce and Jennie Roman, who made their vital editorial contributions at quicksilver pace. We are deeply grateful to Liz Cross for spearheading the book's progress, from start to finish, and to David Fickling for dreaming up this approach to non-fiction, then trusting us to get on and do it. Michael Holyoke's support in making this non-fiction project a reality has been crucial. Thanks also to the wider DFB team, including Bron, Rob, Phil, Rosie, Meggie, Jasmine and Rachel for all their hard work behind the scenes. Huge thanks to Jonathan Stoye for sharing his deep expertise and for his swift turnaround, and to Paul Nurse for his enduring support and for writing such a generous foreword.

BM: I'm intensely grateful to my whole family for all their encouragement, patience and love, but especially to Cal. It's no exaggeration to say this book would not exist without her.

About the Author and Illustrator

Ben Martynoga is a biologist and science writer. After a decade in the lab exploring the insides of brain cells, he swapped his white coat for a pen. Since then he has written about everything from the latest tech innovations to rewilding, running, stress, creativity, microbes and the history of science. Always aiming to make scientific research as clear and relevant as possible, he publishes and edits books, articles, blogs, videos and podcasts. He loves talking about science – and why it matters – with children and adults alike at science festivals, in classrooms or anywhere else. His writing appears in the *Guardian*, *New Statesman*, the *i*, the *Financial Times* and beyond. He lives, works, wanders and wonders (often all at once) in the Lake District.

Moose Allain is an artist, illustrator and prolific tweeter who lives and works in south-west England. He runs workshops and has published a book and an online guide to drawing and colouring, all aiming to inspire children to write and draw. Always on the lookout for interesting projects, his work has encompassed co-producing the video for the band Elbow's 'Lost Worker Bee' single and designing murals for a beauty salon in Mexico City – he's even been tempted to try his hand at stand-up comedy. Moose's cartoons regularly feature in the UK's *Private Eye* magazine.